STOTTLEMYER

HERITAGE BOOKS
AN IMPRINT OF HERITAGE BOOKS, INC.

Books, CDs, and more—Worldwide

For our listing of thousands of titles see our website
at
www.HeritageBooks.com

Published 2007 by
HERITAGE BOOKS, INC.
Publishing Division
65 East Main Street
Westminster, Maryland 21157-5026

International Standard Book Number: 978-0-7884-0923-3

Our Maryland Heritage

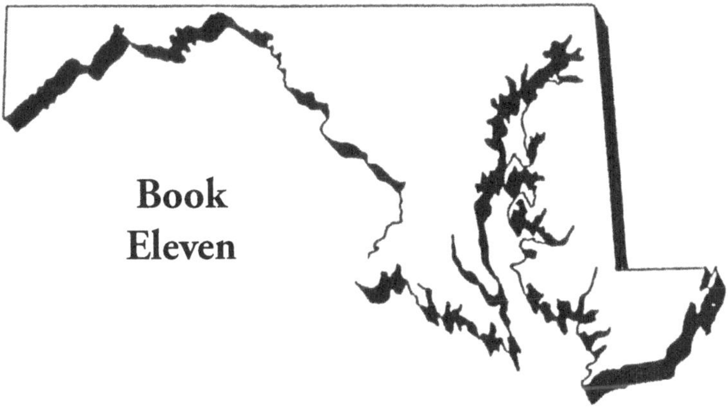

Book
Eleven

The Stottlemyer Families

William N. Hurley, Jr.

HERITAGE BOOKS
2007

ALSO BY W. N. HURLEY, JR.

Available from the publisher: Heritage Books, Inc.

Neikirk-Newkirk-Nikirk, Volume 1

Neikirk-Newkirk-Nikirk, Volume 2

Hurley Families in America, Volume 1

Hurley Families in America, Volume 2

John William Hines 1600, And His Descendants

Maddox, A Southern Maryland Family

Pratt Families of Virginia and Associated Families

Lowder Families in America

Our Maryland Heritage Series:

Book One: The Fry Families
Book Two: The Walker Families
Book Three: The Fulks Families
Book Four: The Watkins Families
Book Five: The King Families
Book Six: The Burdette Families
Book Seven: The Soper Families
Book Eight: The Brandenburg Families
Book Nine: The Purdum Families
Book Ten: The Perry Families

INTRODUCTION

This is the eleventh in our series of families having their origins in Maryland, with descendants now found in all sections of the United States. This study of the Stottlemyer families has been limited somewhat to those members of the family having their origins primarily in Frederick County, Maryland, although others will be mentioned as they are found in other locations.

As will be seen, the Stottlemyers were among the early German settlers of western Maryland. The Stottlemyer family is a very ancient one, with its origins in Germany and Holland. Like many other families with Germanic names, it has undergone many changes in the way it is spelled and, even today, in the same geographic locations, various groups of the family spell their name differently. For the most part, we have found the familiar Stottlemyer, and we have reported it that way in our study, although there have been exceptions.

The family is found very early in the history of the Lower Rhine in Germany. In the seventeenth century, this area was under the control of a Count Palatine, granted such authority by the German Emperor; hence the designation of the inhabitants as Palatines. The Stottlemyer family members (by whatever spelling), were generally members of the Reformed Church, and suffered much from religious persecution. The political leader of the Palatines was Conrad Weiser and the religious leader was the Reverend Joshua Kockerthal. Very early a petition was presented to the King to address the grievances of the Palatines against the Albanians, which was delivered to Conrad Weiser. The outcome of the effort was the violent enmity of the Governor, who attempted to hang all those involved in the petition. As a result, and after suffering the ravages of the Thirty Years War, religious persecution by the French Jesuits, destruction and plunder by King Louis XIV, and an unusually severe winter of 1707/08, many of them immigrated to England, seeking freedom and protection. Apparently that was not very successful, and in 1708 the Reverend Joshua Kockerthal petitioned the London Board of Trade to be sent to America. The result of that petition, and later assistance from Queen Anne, was the great migration of thousands of Palatines, first to New Jersey in 1708, and in 1709 and 1710 to Manhattan Island, as well as the port of Philadelphia, in Pennsylvania, where many of them settled, first in Tolpehocken in Bucks County, and then in areas around that first settlement. The area is now known as the Pennsylvania Dutch country, with its center being Reading.

The map of the central colonies, prepared in 1751 by Colonel Joshua Fry and Peter Jefferson, clearly shows the route of the Great Philadelphia Wagon Road, which led from the port city westerly across the bottom of Pennsylvania, into the western mountains of Maryland at about Hagerstown. It probably followed one of the old Indian trading routes, or an old buffalo trail, as did many early roads. From there, the traveler could move on into the Ohio country, or turn south down the great Shenandoah Valley of Virginia, still following the Wagon Road, all the way to Charlotte, in North Carolina. Many colonists followed that route, seeking new lands, and many of them settled along the way. Many of the Germans among them found the broad valleys of Maryland near Middletown and west of Frederick to their liking, and many of them settled there.

The Stottlemyers were among them, and our story will deal with some of the family found in the area that became Frederick County in 1743.

As colonists continued to arrive in the early years, seven original counties were formed in Maryland under the Colonial Governor: being Anne Arundel; Charles; Kent; Somerset; St. Mary's; Calvert; and Talbot. As settlers moved steadily westward, and took up new lands, it was necessary to form new centers of government to serve them and, over time, sixteen new counties were formed from the original seven, as well as the City of Baltimore. The researcher must be familiar with this formation, in order to know the sources of information for any given time-frame. The following tabulation demonstrates the formation of each of the counties of Maryland:

Formation of the Counties of Maryland

Name of County	Formed	Source County or Counties
Allegany	1789	Washington
Anne Arundel	1650	Original County
Baltimore	1660	Anne Arundel
Calvert	1654	Original County
Caroline	1773	Dorchester & Queen Anne's
Carroll	1837	Baltimore & Frederick
Cecil	1674	Baltimore & Kent
Charles	1658	Original County
Dorchester	1669	Somerset & Talbot
Frederick	1748	Prince George's & Baltimore
Garrett	1872	Allegany
Harford	1773	Baltimore
Howard	1851	Anne Arundel
Kent	1642	Original County
Montgomery	1776	Frederick
Prince George's	1695	Calvert & Charles
Queen Anne's	1706	Dorchester, Kent & Talbot
Somerset	1666	Original County
St. Mary's	1637	Original County
Talbot	1662	Original County
Washington	1776	Frederick
Wicomico	1867	Somerset & Worcester
Worcester	1742	Somerset

ORDER OF PRESENTATION

Our studies deal primarily with descendants of one distinct ancestral individual, David Stottlemyer, born in Munich, Germany. He reportedly arrived in the colonies August 11, 1750 aboard the *Patience,* Hugh Steel, Captain, out of Rotterdam. Said by some to be the ancestor of all the Stottlemyers in America - a rather sweeping claim - his descendants are found in both Frederick and Montgomery Counties of Maryland, as well as other states.

First, in Chapter 1, we will discuss the descendants of David, who died in Frederick County in 1791, leaving extensive records of his passing, and twelve children. The information available as to their descendants, in both the male and female lineage, will be presented in that chapter, with the exception of two of his sons about whom we know much more.

Chapter 2 will concern itself with a similar study of the lineage of George Stottlemyer, one of the sons of David, The Immigrant.

Chapter 3 will present the descendants of yet another son of David, The Immigrant; David Stottlemyer, Jr.

In Chapter 4, we will discuss the descendants of Daniel Stottlemyer, who was a son of David, Jr., and a grandson of David Stottlemyer, The Immigrant.

Chapter 5 will be devoted to the rather extensive family of Rose Anna Stottlemyer, who was a daughter of Daniel, and a great granddaughter of David, The Immigrant.

These first five chapters will deal solely with those persons known to have been descended from David Stottlemyer, the original Immigrant to America, who arrived in 1750. We will here be discussing numerous generations to the present date, in both male and female lineages.

Finally, the last two chapters are devoted to some general information about Stottlemyers found in Frederick and Washington Counties, who have not been placed within the framework of the families discussed, although they perhaps belong there.

The work is followed by a Bibliography of sources searched, and an all-name, every page, index.

CONTENTS

David Stottlemyer
Born Germany
died c.1791
The Immigrant

*
*
* * * * * *
*
* * George Stottlemyer, Sr. .... Chapter 2
*
* * Jacob Stottlemyer
*
* * John Stottlemyer
*
* * David Stottlemyer, Jr. .... Chapter 3
*
* * Mary Ann Catherine Stottlemyer
*
* * Eve Magdalena Stottlemyer
*
* * Catherine Elizabeth Stottlemyer
*
* * Elizabeth Stottlemyer
*
* * Hamilton Jefferson Stottlemyer
*
* * Benjamin Stottlemyer
*
* * Joseph Stottlemyer
*
* * Dewalt Stottlemyer

CHAPTER 1

David Stottlemyer
The Immigrant
died c.1791

This appears to be one of the earliest members of the family that we have been able to identify in Frederick County.

History of Frederick County Maryland, by T. J. C. Williams, in Volume II, reports that David was born and educated in Munich, Germany, and came to Maryland as a young man, where he became one of the earliest settlers of the Middletown valley in Frederick, County. The report also states that he was married and had five children, one of whom was another David. At the time the book was written (in 1910), several of the children were deceased, but as will be seen from the following study, there were as many as twelve children in the family, including the second David.

Another report, found in the family file in the Frederick County Historical Society library, author unknown, states that David arrived in America August 11, 1750 aboard the ship *Patience*, Hugh Steel, Captain, from Rotterdam, last from Cowes. The report also claims, rather boldly, that David is the ancestor of **all** the American Stottlemyers (emphasis added).

On March 10, 1761, David obtained a deed from one Nicholas Fink, recorded in Liber F, at folio 1260 in the Frederick County land records. The deed was for 50 acres of the tract called *Resurvey on Prevention*, for a consideration of 25 pounds, current money. On May 3, 1765, David conveyed what appears to be the same land back to Nicholas Fink by deed recorded in Liber J at folio 1144. It is there stated that the consideration is that Fink is conveying to David a tract of 50 acres, being part of *Goose Bill*, in exhange for this property, by deed of the same date, recorded in Liber J at folio 1142. David is described as being a miller, and his wife's name appears as Mary in the acknowledgment to the deed.

David's will appears in Will Book GM-2 at folio 371 among the Frederick County records. There, he names his wife, Mary, to receive his real and personal property for her lifetime, or until she should remarry. On the happening of either, the estate is to be sold and divided equally between his sons and daughters, named in the will. The Executors were his wife, Mary, and Jacob Alexander of Henry. The will was entered for record March 14, 1791.

There is also the will of Magdalene Stottlemyer, naming the same group of children, which is probably the widow of David, perhaps with a proper name of Mary Magdalene. It is dated January 23, 1813 and entered for record February 22, 1813 in Liber RB-1 at folio 363. The will also mentions a grandson, Jacob Alexander, Jr., as the sole Executor. The children will first be listed, not necessarily in order, and then where there is significant information, two of the children will be assigned to succeeding chapters, and one (the last listed) will be discussed in greater detail here following:

1. George Stottlemyer, Sr., of whom more in Chapter 2.
2. Jacob Stottlemyer; the same Jacob reported on a marriage license dated January 25, 1785 in Frederick County to Hedwick Shoemaker.
3. John Stottlemyer; believed to be the same John reported on a married license dated July 27, 1798 in Frederick County, Maryland to Sarah Michael.
4. David Stottlemyer, Jr., of whom more in Chapter 3.
5. Mary Ann Catherine Stottlemyer, born in Frederick County, Maryland. She was called Mary in her mother's will. Apparently she married Jacob Alexander of Henry, and was the mother of:
    a. Jacob Alexander, Jr.
6. Eve Magdalena Stottlemyer; married to Lenhart.

7. Catherine Elizabeth Stottlemyer; married Hargessheimer.
8. Elizabeth Stottlemyer; married to Siferd.
9. Hamilton Jefferson Stottlemyer. This individual is included as a son of David Stottlemyer, the Immigrant, and born in Frederick County, Maryland, although he is not mentioned in the will of either of his parents. His inclusion is based on the will of Benjamin Stottlemyer, probated October 16, 1841 (see following), in which Benjamin mentions his brother, Hamilton Jefferson, as well as his nephew, Benjamin Stottlemyer, son of Duvault Stottlemyer, who must also be a brother.
10. Benjamin Stottlemyer, born in Frederick County, Maryland, and died during 1841 in Washington County. His will, dated October 15, 1841, and probated the next day, is filed in Book D at folio 459 in the will records of the county. The will was executed in Fairfield County, Ohio, and probated there; and indexed in Washington County, Maryland, due to bequests involving land in that county. The will names his wife, Pamela, as principal legatee during her lifetime, including references to a farm located in Washington County. He also mentions a brother, Hamilton Jefferson Stottlemyer, and a nephew, Benjamin Stottlemyer, son of Duvault Stottlemyer, relative to a tract of land in Washington County along the Potomac River, known as *Ettings Right.* There are no children mentioned in the will.
11. Joseph Stottlemyer, perhaps. Later family members have been reported to have said that there was a Joseph who went to Virginia as a young man.
12. Dewalt (or Duvault) Stottlemyer, of whom more.

Dewalt Stottlemyer

This son of David Stottlemyer, the Immigrant, was born in Frederick County, Maryland. He also appears as Devault and Duvault Stottlemyer, and is perhaps the same individual who appears in numerous entries in land records of Washington County, Maryland, from 1839 to 1867. Records indicate that on November 27, 1860, a meeting was held in the town of Hancock, Washington County, to discuss the position western Marylanders would take in the coming struggle between the states. Devault Stottlemyer was one of the three members of a committee appointed to prepare a series of resolutions, which were unanimously adopted, declaring their trust and belief in the National Government. The report found in the Historical Society states that Duvault (there spelled Dewalt) was married July 22, 1794 to Barbara Bossert. At the Historical Society library in Hagerstown, I found a letter from Rosalie Doyle Siri, dated during February, 1985, inquiring as to the Stottlemyer family, as well as the families of Doyle, Wilkinson, Wolverton and Rummell. She stated Duvault was the father of, at least:

1. Robert Fulton Stottlemyer, born c.1831 in Maryland; married January 19, 1859 in Washington County, Amelia Catherine Wolverton. Three children:
    a. Lavinia Stottlemyer, born c.1868 in Maryland; died 1939. She was married c.1888 to Amos Bender Wilkinson.
    b. Virginia Stottlemyer.
    c. John D. Stottlemyer
2. Benjamin F. Stottlemyer, as mentioned in the will of his uncle, for whom he was apparently named. Died in 1842 in Fairfield County, Ohio; single.
3. Duvault Stottlemyer, Jr. Married Lovina West and had children, born at Hancock, Maryland:
    a. Benjamin F. Stottlemyer, married to Elizabeth Gill; second to Elizabeth Rhodes and third to Lucy Parrish. He had children; five to his first marriage, three to the second, and perhaps two to the third:
        (1) Mildred B. Stottlemyer.

(2) George B. Stottlemyer.
(3) Benjamin Stottlemyer.
(4) Bertie Stottlemyer.
(5) Anne Lou Stottlemyer.
(6) Wallace Stottlemyer.
(7) Cora Stottlemyer.
(8) Duvault Stottlemyer.
(9) John D. Stottlemyer.
(10) Verne Stottlemyer.

b. Wasson Stottlemyer, married May 23, 1865 at Hagerstown, Maryland, to Minerva Brosius. They had children:
(1) Charles Stottlemyer.
(2) Robert Stottlemyer.
(3) Edward Stottlemyer.
(4) Raymond Stottlemyer.
(5) Walter Stottlemyer.

c. Elizabeth Stottlemyer, married Walter Frost Crane.

d. Mercena Stottlemyer, married Jacob Bower, and had children:
(1) Louis Bower.
(2) Ike Bower.
(3) Ada Bower.
(4) Mollie Bower.
(5) Benjamin Bower.

e. Fulton Stottlemyer, married to Kate and second to Henrietta B.

4. Hamilton Jefferson Stottlemyer.

David Stottlemyer
Born Germany
died c.1791
The Immigrant
*
*

George Stottlemyer, Sr.
*

*   *   *   *   *   *
*
* * Elizabeth Stottlemyer 1791-1873
*
* * George Stottlemyer, Jr. 1793-1871
*
* * John Poe Stottlemyer 1796-1879
*
* * Nelson Stottlemyer 1802-1860
*
* * Madeline Stottlemyer
*
* * Daughter Stottlemyer

CHAPTER 2

George Stottlemyer, Sr.

This son of David Stottlemyer, the Immigrant, was born in Frederick County, Maryland, and married Rebecca Harriet Poe, born c.1760, daughter of George Poe. Children:

1. Elizabeth Stottlemyer. We believe this to be the same individual who was born c.1791 in Frederick County and died January 1, 1873 at the age of 82 years and 3 days. She was married November 19, 1811 to Levin Hurley, born c.1787 in Frederick County and died there on August 26, 1863 at the age of 76 years, 2 months and 24 days. He was the son of Moses Hurley (1750-1842). The will of Moses can be found in will book GME-2 at page 722 in Frederick County, Maryland. We can not now prove the connection, but Moses could easily have moved to Frederick County from one of the eastern counties of Maryland, as other members of the Hurley family did. In his will, Moses does not mention the name of his wife, but I was rather impressed with the thoughts set forth, and repeat them here: "*Whereas the property which I now possess both real and personal hath been chiefly acquired by the joint industry and frugality of my dear wife and myself the better to enable her to live with convenience and comfort, I do therefore give and bequeath unto my said wife during her natural life all my property both real and personal except what is hereafter mentioned.*" A rather unusual attitude for that day and time, expressing a great deal of affection. The will then proceeds to describe a number of specific bequests to his various children, after the death of their mother. The 1850 census of Frederick County, Maryland, carries the family of Levin and Elizabeth, listing three children still

at home. Levin, Jr. was then about 23, and not included. Also in the household was Sarah Magruder, born c.1835, not otherwise identified. The children were:

a. Uriah W. Hurley, born c.1825

b. Levin Hurley, Jr., born 1827 in Frederick County, Maryland and died there February 8, 1902 at the age of 74 years, 2 months and 3 days. He was married in the county on June 3, 1857 to Mary Ann E. Morrison. She was born c.1833 and died March 17, 1913 at the age of 79 years, 7 months and 23 days. Mormon Church family group sheets list him as Levi and his wife as Mary Ann Munson, born June 24, 1833, daughter of Lewis and Elizabeth Swope Munson. The children are the same in all records, so we are here dealing with the same individuals, in spite of the name differences. The will of Levin Hurley, Jr. is found in will book CES-1 at page 273 in Frederick County records, dated September 19, 1901, and admitted for probate March 3, 1902. It is witnessed by Irving Stottlemyer, Thomas F. Grossnickle and Charles C. Grossnickle. The will is quite simple, leaving the entire estate to his wife for her lifetime, and then to be divided among his three children:

    (1) Mary Ellen Hurley, born February 18, 1859; married to Stottlemyer, perhaps Irving

    (2) Amanda E. Hurley, born February 19, 1861; married to Kelbaugh

    (3) Celia Ann Catherine Hurley, born November 21, 1863, and married to Lewis.

c. Lewis Hurley, born c.1828

d. John E. Hurley, born c.1835

2. George Stottlemyer, Jr., born c.1793 and died October 6, 1871 at the age of 78 years, 3 months and 2 days. He is buried at the Wolfsville United Brethren Church, with his wife. She was Susan, born c.1795, died June 5, 1872,

"about the age of 77 years." The will of George was dated June 1, 1871 and entered for probate November 27, 1871, recorded in Book SGC-1 at folio 213 in Frederick County, Maryland. Witnesses to his will were David Biser, Henry F. C. Stottlemyer and David M. Bickerstaff. Henry F. C. Stottlemyer was a son of Daniel Stottlemyer, who died in 1874. Daniel was a son of David Stottlemyer, Jr. (1794), who was a brother of George Stottlemyer, Sr. Therefore, if we are correct in placing this George, Jr., then his will was witnessed by his nephew (Henry F. C.). Further, Daniel A. Biser was married to Rose Ann Stottlemyer, a sister of Henry F. C. Stottlemyer, so there is a relationship with the Biser family as well. George left to his daughter, Susan, one cow, one bed and bedstead, "to make her even with my other daughters which are married and have already gotten that amount," but fails to name the other daughters. The residue is left to his wife, also named Susan, without mention of any other heirs. The onc child identified was:

a. Susan Stottlemyer.

3. John Poe Stottlemyer, of whom more
4. Nelson Stottlemyer, born May 7, 1802, died September 30, 1860 and is buried at Wolfsville United Brethren Church, in Frederick County, Maryland. He was reportedly married July 25, 1820 to Hannah Pryor in Washington County. She is buried with her husband, and was born c.1802, died December 25, 1862, at the age of 60 years, 9 months and 23 days. One son is buried with them; there may have been other children:

   a. Joshua P. Stottlemyer, born 1844, died August 28, 1852
5. Madeline Stottlemyer.
6. Daughter Stottlemyer.

John Poe Stottlemyer
1796-1879

John Poe was born February 26, 1796, died April 9, 1879, and is buried at the Ellerton Brethren Church. Records of the Mormon Church indicate that he was a son of George Stottlemyer, Sr. and Rebecca Harriet Poe (1760), daughter of George Poe. Married to Susannah Rebecca Wolfe, born 1803, died June 19, 1885, daughter of David Wolfe, Sr. and Nancy Matilda Hauver. The will of John Poe is dated November 20, 1865 and entered for record May 6, 1879 in will book JRR1 at folio 400, Frederick County. He left the home farm of 83 acres to his wife, Susan, and various bequests to his children, and to a grandchild named Ida Stottlemyer. In the Orphans Court records of May 3, 1879, the heirs affirm that their father had intended to include Nancy Grossnickle as one of his heirs, and it appears that all of the children signed that request. From these records, and from the census of 1850 for Frederick County, the children included:

1. Caroline Stottlemyer, the eldest daughter, married to John Bowman. They lived in Ogle County, Ohio, and had at least two daughters:
    a. Nancy J. Bowman, born 1846, died March 9, 1896. Married to John T. Harshman of Frederick County, born October 30, 1841 near Wolfsville, Maryland, died August 7, 1908 at his home in Myersville. The son of John Harshman and Elizabeth Grossnickle, John T. is buried at the German Baptist Church near Ellerton. Nine children, seven of whom reached maturity, born on the family farm near Wolfsville, about a quarter of a mile west of the town, on the Boonsboro Road:
        (1) Upton W. Harshman, born November 22, 1866 near Wolfsville. After graduation from Lebanon Valley College, Annville, Pa., he be-

gan a teaching career in Wolfsville. In 1890, he became principal of the public schools in Ringgold, Maryland, serving there for six years. In 1898, he purchased the Joseph M. Bell farm, consisting of 120 acres located three miles southwest of Waynesboro, Franklin County, Pennsylvania. In 1906 he purchased the C. W. Reichard fruit farm in Washington County, Maryland, and in 1909, the adjoining Abram Mickley farm, until he had more than 250 acres in fruit trees. Married E. May Rowe of Ringgold, youngest daughter of Daniel Rowe and Nancy Gehr. They had two sons.

(2) Flora May Harshman, born c.1867, died November 29, 1871 at just under four years old.

(3) Mary E. Harshman, born c.1869, died July 24, 1870

(4) Ira V. Harshman, a farmer in Catoctin District

(5) Aquilla A. Harshman, born July 25, 1873, died July 28, 1932; buried at Ellerton Brethren Church. As a young man, he purchased a small truck farm near Ellerton. Married to Jennie C. Cartee, born May 24, 1876, died June 28, 1937, daughter of Frisby G. Cartee (1846) and Louisa C. Grossnickle (1850). Five children:
   (a) J. Frank Harshman.
   (b) Wilbur C. Harshman.
   (c) Millard A. Harshman, a twin.
   (d) May L. Harshman, a twin.
   (e) Nancy Harshman.

(6) Annie A. Harshman, born 1876, died 1942. Married John F. Harshman (not a relative) of Middletown, born 1870, died 1957. Both are buried at Ellerton Brethren Church.

(7) Alvey P. Harshman, born February 22, 1878, remaining on the family farm until he obtained a farm near Boonsboro, in Washington County. After a few years there, he returned to Frederick County and bought the family farm from his father. Married to Minnie A. Hooper, the daughter of John William Hooper (1862) and Lucretia Shuff (1862). One son:
    (a) John W. Harshman.
(8) Sallie M. Harshman, married Sherman Clark, a farmer of Beaver Creek, Washington County
(9) J. Lloyd Harshman, who graduated from Juniata College at Huntingdon, Pennsylvania.

b. Cynthia Bowman.

2. Pointon Stottlemyer, born c.1825, died April 5, 1886 at age 61 years, 3 months; buried Wolfsville Reformed Church. Married to Margaret Jane, born c.1831, died January 24, 1890 at age 59 years, 11 months, 24 days. He left a will, dated April 4, 1886, probated April 19, 1886 and recorded in will book JPP2 at folio 239, in Frederick County. He names his wife, and six children:
    a. Susan Stottlemyer.
    b. Edward Stottlemyer.
    c. David Arthur Stottlemyer.
    d. Harvey L. Stottlemyer.
    e. Lemuel C. Stottlemyer.
    f. Clara J. Stottlemyer.
3. Susan Stottlemyer, born c.1829, died June 16, 1900 at the age of 70 years, 7 months and 29 days. Certificate of marriage dated February 14, 1851 Frederick County to Hezekiah Palmer, born c.1827, died May 1, 1913 at the age of 86 years, 7 months and 8 days. Both are buried at Ellerton Brethren Church.
4. Nancy G. Stottlemyer, born March 11, 1832, died October 5, 1888. Certificate of marriage dated January 22,

1851 in Frederick County, to Elias Grossnickle, born April 18, 1829 in Frederick County, died June 2, 1912; son of Peter Grossnickle (1786) and Rebecca Margaret Hauver (1790). They had children, born in Frederick County, including:

a. Charles Upton Grossnickle, a twin, born August 16, 1856, died October 28, 1957. In 1902 he purchased the 136-acres farm of his father, where he had been born. In 1909, he bought a second farm of 170 acres from Daniel Grossnickle, located two miles east of Ellerton, neal Hyland, Maryland. Married February 1, 1881 to Mary Elizabeth Toms, born October 18, 1861, died May 19, 1884, daughter of Ezra Toms (1826) and Sophia Doub (1829). She is buried at the German Baptist Church; they had two children. After her death, he married secondly in 1887 to Ella Leatherman, daughter of Daniel Leatherman and Caroline Michael. There were ten children born to this second marriage, nine of whom lived to maturity. Children of Charles Upton Grossnickle were:
   (1) Nannie May Grossnickle, born November 3, 1881, died January 23, 1978; married Milton A. Summers.
   (2) An infant death.
   (3) Upton W. Grossnickle.
   (4) Carrie Grossnickle, married Foster Leatherman.
   (5) Daisy U. Grossnickle.
   (6) Raymond Grossnickle.
   (7) Daniel R. Grossnickle.
   (8) Nellie N. Grossnickle.
   (9) Bertie G. Grossnickle.
   (10) Robert G. Grossnickle.
   (11) Paul Grossnickle.

b. Clara E. Grossnickle, a twin; August 16, 1856. Married to the Reverend Silas Harp.

c. Susan Rebecca Grossnickle, born c.1852, died June 10, 1909 at age 57 years, 5 months and 10 days. Married John C. Leatherman, born December 15, 1852, near Petersville in Frederick County, died January 25, 1952, the son of George Leatherman (1827) and Rebecca E. Johnson. Susan and John are buried at Ellerton Brethren Church. John C. Leatherman was a prosperous farmer, and a wealthy man: a stockholder in the Farmers Exchange of Myersville; the Washington Realty Company; and in the Flook, Gavers, Summers, Leatherman and Grossnickle Bank of Myersville, of which he was also a director. Children:
   (1) Vernon Ward Leatherman, born 1874. Married to Florence E. Harshman, born 1874, died 1952. Both buried at Ellerton Brethren Church
   (2) George U. Leatherman, married to Adie C. Harshman.
   (3) Roy L. Leatherman, married Vada E. Grossnickle.
   (4) Nannie R. Leatherman, married to John W. Eldridge of Gary, Indiana.
   (5) Clare E. Leatherman.

5. Rebecca Stottlemyer, born March 21, 1834, died June 27, 1887; buried at St. Paul's Church in the former village of Utica Mills, Frederick County. Certificate of marriage dated December 29, 1860 in Frederick County, to Albert J. Cramer, born April 26, 1832 in Frederick and died January 9, 1871, son of Eli Cramer (1796) and Phebe Ellis (1801). Children, born at Creagerstown District, Frederick:

   a. Mabel Cramer, born c.1861
   b. Charles Cramer, born about 1863

c. George Cramer, born about 1867

d. Eli D. Cramer, born about 1869, died 1952. Married to Julia A., born 1870, died 1942. Both buried at the cemetery of the old village of Utica Mills

6. John W. Stottlemyer, born c.1827 and died August 26, 1901 at the age of 74 years, 9 months and 7 days. Buried at Myersville United Brethren Church with his wife. He was married November 23, 1847 to Mary Helen Roback, born c.1829, died April 21, 1894 at the age of 65 years 2 months, 17 days. One son is buried with them; there could have been others:

   a. Noah E. Stottlemyer, born c.1848, died June 27, 1866 at the age of 18 years, 9 days.

7. Franklin Stottlemyer, born February 7, 1840, died July 30, 1917; buried Lutheran Church near former village of Utica Mills. Married to Maria Jane Jackson, by license dated June 25, 1862 in Frederick County. She was born May 16, 1846, died August 12, 1935; buried with her husband. His will was found in Book SD-2 at folio 400, dated February 24, 1911 and proven August 9, 1917 in Frederick County. The will refers to a wife and six children, although only three sons are mentioned by name. Maria Jane left a will probated January 6, 1935, recorded in will book MFS 1 at folio 598, Frederick County. She was much more specific than her husband, naming not only her children, but grandchildren as well. From her will, we can construct the family:

   a. Clarence W. Stottlemyer. His father's will provided that Clarence should have the right to buy a certain farm from the estate. By document dated September 25, 1917 and recorded in will book SDT 2 at folio 439, Clarence exercised that right, buying the tract of 76 acres in the village of Utica, Lewistown District of Frederick County. This is probably the same Clarence W. Stottlemyer who was born February 2,

1876, and is buried at the Lutheran Church in the former village of Utica Mills. His wife, Estella, is buried there also, born August 6, 1881.

b. George F. Stottlemyer. He was deceased prior to the making of his mother's will, leaving children, named in the will. He is probably the same George F. who was born 1865 and died October 28, 1918; buried at Rocky Ridge Brethren Church with his wife. Married to Phoebe A. Whitmore, d/o David Whitmore (1812) and Martha M. Hospilhorn. She was born May 20, 1865 and died November 14, 1929. The children named in the will were:
   (1) Clarence B. Stottlemyer.
   (2) Martha J. Stottlemyer.
   (3) David F. Stottlemyer.
   (4) Laura Stottlemyer.
   (5) Carrie Stottlemyer.

c. Henry Stottlemyer. This is the same Henry who is buried at the Lutheran Church near the old village of Utica Mills (where his parents are buried). He was born May 25, 1870, died April 22, 1946. His wife was Effie Irene, born March 20, 1876. Under the terms of the will of Henry's mother, Effie received the large split-bottom rocking chair. Henry's will, written near Utica in Frederick County, dated March 19, 1945, was probated May 13, 1946 and recorded in will book RLL2 at folio 282 in Frederick County. It names his wife, one son and one daughter:
   (1) Franklin H. Stottlemyer, who received his father's mantel clock, with wooden works in it, as well as the home farm and the Brengle farm containing about 179 acres.
   (2) Alta Irene Stottlemyer, married to Hubbard. She received the 140-acres Summers farm.

d. Rosa Catherine Stottlemyer, born October 23, 1871, died August 20, 1933. Married to Samuel B. Martz, born September 6, 1866, died December 3, 1933, son of Lewis J. Martz (1836) and Margaret C. Staley (1844). Rosie and Samuel are buried at Mt. Olivet Cemetery in Frederick. They lived on a farm of 158 and 1/2 acres purchased from the estate of Thomas Geesey, located near Lake View in the Lewistown District, about eight miles north of the city of Frederick. She was deceased prior to the death of her mother, leaving five children, mentioned in the will:
   (1) Lola Jane Martz, married John Blackston.
   (2) Louis F. Martz.
   (3) Clarence H. Martz.
   (4) Allen B. Martz.
   (5) Mary Martz, married Clarence Warner.

e. Emma Lee Stottlemyer, born c.1863, died March 25, 1950 at the age of 87 years, 3 months and 28 days. Married to Charles T. B. Albaugh, born 1867, died 1940. Both buried at the cemetery in old Utica Mills.

f. Mary Stottlemyer, born 1874. Married to Ernest K. Harper, born 1872, died 1936. Buried at cemetery at old Utica Mills.

8. Cynthia A. Stottlemyer; married to Parker.

David Stottlemyer
Born Germany
died c.1791
The Immigrant
*
*

David Stottlemyer, Jr.
died c.1821
*

*   *   *   *   *   *
*
*   * Jacob Stottlemyer
*
*   * John McGruder Stottlemyer
*
*   * Elizabeth Stottlemyer
*
*   * Daniel Stottlemyer 1796-1864 ....Chapter 4
*
*   * David Stottlemyer, III 1794-1865
*
*   * Joseph Stottlemyer 1797-1864
*
*   * Polly Stottlemyer
*
*   * Margaret Agnes Stottlemyer

CHAPTER 3

David Stottlemyer, Jr.
died c.1821

This son of David Stottlemyer (died c.1791), the Immigrant, was born in old Frederick County, Maryland, probably c.1787 (assuming an age of twenty-one years at the time of his marriage). He was married to Margaret McGruder (in later generations probably anglicized to Magruder), and his will, dated January 6, 1821, was entered for record February 19, 1821, recorded in Book HS-2 at folio 439. In the will, he leaves one third of his estate to his wife, but does not list her name. He then leaves the plantation, consisting of 15 acres of *Baker's Lot* and 134 acres of *Peace Approaching*, to his three sons: Daniel, David and Joseph. After the death of his wife, these three sons have six years to pay certain bequests to the other children, also named in the will. Also mentioned in the will is one John Webb, who was to receive twenty-five dollars, or a colt worth that amount, when he reached the age of twenty-one. He is not further identified. The Executors are two of his sons; David and Daniel. Witnesses were Levin Hurley, George Stottlemyer and Nelson Stottlemyer. Some of the children of this family are found in the marriage records of Washington County, Maryland, suggesting that the family, or some of the children, may have moved there. The children of David named in his will included:

1. Jacob Stottlemyer, a twin, of whom more as Child 1.
2. John McGruder Stottlemyer, a twin, who received two hundred dollars under his father's will, and was perhaps married in Washington County to Susanna Wolf by certificate dated November 19, 1819. John is reportedly the founder of the town of Myersville, Maryland, and was perhaps also married October 10, 1832 to Henrietta

Hays. Children, apparently the first born to the first marriage, and the rest to the second:

a. Cassianus Stottlemyer, born c.1826, died December 5, 1901 at age 75 years, 2 days. Buried Wolfsville United Brethren Church. Married December 5, 1861 to Caroline Smith, daughter of John Smith, Jr. and Catherine Garnand.
b. Mathias Stottlemyer.
c. Jackson Stottlemyer.
d. Thomas J. Stottlemyer.
e. Martin V. B. Stottlemyer.
f. Mary Ann Stottlemyer.
g. Malinda Stottlemyer.

3. Elizabeth Stottlemyer, the eldest daughter, who received one hundred dollars under the will. Married September 2, 1819 in Washington County to Owen Forrest.
4. Daniel Stottlemyer, born 1796, and of whom more in Chapter 4.
5. David Stottlemyer, III, born c.1794, died February 28, 1865. Married to Isabella Hays by certificate dated February 17, 1825 in Washington County. She was born July 9, 1806, died January 27, 1870; they had children:
   a. Isaiah Stottlemyer.
   b. David Stottlemyer.
   c. Hiram Stottlemyer.
   d. Jemima Stottlemyer.
   e. Susan Stottlemyer, married John H. Johnson.
   f. Elizabeth Stottlemyer.
6. Joseph Stottlemyer, married in Washington County to Sophia Hays by certificate dated January 16, 1835. This is believed to be the same Joseph who was born c.1797 and died March 29, 1864 at the age of sixty-seven years. Buried at Wolfsville Lutheran Church, Frederick County. His wife Margaret Ann Sophia is buried with him; she was born c.1820 and died September 1, 1856 at the age

of thirty-six years, ten months and four days. There are two sons buried with them; there could be others:

a. Manfred Stottlemyer, born 1852, died March 18, 1858 at the age of 5 years, 11 months and 14 days.
b. James Stottlemyer, born 1856, died October 30, 1856 at the age of 6 months and 29 days.

7. Polly Stottlemyer, the youngest daughter, who also received one hundred dollars, plus one cow and one bedstead and bedding.
8. Margaret Agnes Stottlemyer, married to George Lizer or Lyzar.

CHILD 1

Jacob Stottlemyer

This son of David Stottlemyer, Jr. (died 1821) and Margaret McGruder, Jacob Stottlemyer, a twin, was married to Barbara Protzman in Washington County by certificate dated October 28, 1815. They had children:

1. Reason Stottlemyer, married Susan; no children.
2. Joshua Stottlemyer, born May 29, 1844. Married Malinda and had children:
   a. Daniel Stottlemyer.
3. Daniel Stottlemyer, born c.1832, probably in Frederick County. Married on July 21, 1854 to Elizabeth Harshman, born c.1835, died June 3, 1893; buried at Ellerton Brethren Church, the daughter of Christian Harshman, III. Children:
   a. Mary Catherine Stottlemyer, born c.1856
   b. James Columbus Stottlemyer, born c.1858, who was probably married April 13, 1879 to Alice R. Brown.
   c. Nathaniel Stottlemyer, born c.1860. Married to Manzella Forrest, born c.1860 in Maryland, and they

had at least four children, probably born at or near Hagerstown, in Washington County, Maryland:

(1) Blanche Stottlemyer, born c.1877
(2) Roy Stottlemyer, born c.1878
(3) Omar Stottlemyer, born c.1879
(4) Esta M. Stottlemyer, born c.1881; died January 9, 1969

d. Sarah Ann Marie Stottlemyer, born c.1861
e. Jacob Christopher Stottlemyer, born c.1863
f. Jonathan Elias Stottlemyer, born c.1865
g. Phoebe Ellen Stottlemyer, born c.1866
h. Amanda Emeline Stottlemyer, born c.1868
i. Andrew Jackson Stottlemyer, born c.1870. This is perhaps the A. J. Stottlemyer who is buried at Germantown Church of God, Fort Richie. He is listed there as born c.1871 and died 1941. His wife, Daisy E., is buried with him; born 1872, died 1956.
j. Eliza Jane Stottlemyer, born c.1872

4. Sally Stottlemyer.
5. Emeline Stottlemyer.
6. Mary Stottlemyer, married Roles.
7. Catharine Stottlemyer, of whom more following.
8. Susan Stottlemyer.

Catharine Stottlemyer

This daughter of Jacob Stottlemyer and Barbara Protzman was married December 8, 1846 at the home of Daniel Derr to Jacob Biser, born January 7, 1823, son of Jacob Biser and Catherine Brandenburg. They had four children:

1. Mary Catherine Biser, born February 16, 1849, and died December 16, 1849. Buried at the Middletown Reformed Church.
2. Lloyd Calvin Biser, born December 30, 1851, died 1917. Married January 2, 1876 in Bates County, Missouru, to

Cynthia A. Johnson, born 1856, died 1932. Known as Cal, he migrated during the 1870s to Missouri with his brother Daniel, where they first settled in Hume, Bates County. Cal had a blacksmith shop there, and he and his wife are buried in the local cemetery. Six children:

a. Will Biser.

b. Walter R. Biser, born 1878, died 1955. Married to Lu Dema, born 1888, died 1965. They lived in St. Joseph, but were buried at Hume cemetery, with his parents and other family members. Three children:

   (1) Olene Biser, married Chuck Jeffers and had at least one child:

      (a) Juni Jeffers, married Ellis.

   (2) Lester Biser.

   (3) Nedra Biser.

c. Rose Biser, born 1884, died 1949. Married Lewis J. Branum, born December 31, 1881, died October 3, 1911. Buried at Hume cemetery; reportedly had two daughters and a son.

d. Nisha G. Biser.

e. Jessie L. Biser.

f. Raymond J. Biser.

3. Sarah Salina Biser, born March 10, 1853, died June 10, 1854. Buried at Middletown Reformed Church cemetery.

4. Daniel Jonas Biser, born June 4, 1856, died July 29, 1928. Married November 18, 1880 in Bates County, Missouri to Ellen Covert, born October 1, 1856, died June 9, 1934. As mentioned above, he migrated during the 1870s with his brother Lloyd Calvin to Hume, and settled there. He had six children:

a. Chester Franklin Biser, born 1881, died 1899

b. Jennie, died as an infant.

c. Roy Hamilton Biser, born September 8, 1885, and of whom more following.

d. Bertha Biser, born 1889, died 1895

e. Orville Ernest Biser, born April 4, 1893, died 1970. Buried in Hume cemetery, Bates County, Missouri. Married twice: first to Grace McClure and second to Edith. He and Grace lived in Kansas City, Missouri, and had two children:
   (1) Vera Biser, married to Dr. Jack B. Caldwell.
   (2) Robert Biser, lived in Springfield, Missouri.

f. Nora Belle Biser, born May 2, 1895 at Hume, Bates County, Missouri; died December 9, 1977. Married George Curtis Forbes, lived in Kansas City, and had one child:
   (1) Evelyn J. Forbes, married Larry Bates and had three children:
      (a) Scott Christopher Bates.
      (b) Greg Kendall Bates, a twin
      (c) Gary Kirkland Bates, a twin

Roy Hamilton Biser
1885-1949

This son of Daniel Jonas Biser (1856) and Ellen Covert (1856) was born September 8, 1885, died September 23, 1949. Married Anna Ruth Mountjoy, born December 31, 1891 in Hall County, Nebraska, died June 27, 1980. Both buried in Clay County, Texas. They had four children:

1. Elisabeth Biser, born June 23, 1919 in Kansas City, Missouri. Married July 29, 1945 Doctor Richard Edgar Jay in Beaumont, Jefferson County, Texas. Two children:
   a. Cathleen Jay, born November 19, 1949. Married to Robert Hall and has at least one son:
      (1) Spenser Hall, born April 5, 1985
   b. Douglas Bruce Jay, born November 18, 1951. Married to Gloria Tripp and had three children:
      (1) Matthew Brandon Jay: September 17, 1978
      (2) Lisa Marie Jay: March 8, 1981

(3) Robert Christopher Jay: August 14, 1983.

2. Margaret Jane Biser, born September 17, 1920 in Butler, Bates County, Missouri. Married June 6, 1942 in Beaumont, Texas, Ralph Weir Kinsey. They lived in Lamesa, Texas, and had four children:
   a. Anna Murphy Kinsey, born April 13, 1945. Married April 7, 1968 to Naaman E. Nickell and had two children, born at Houston, Texas:
      (1) Dawn Angela Nickell: January 17, 1970
      (2) Amber Lynn Nickell: September 14, 1971
   b. Elisabeth Jane Kinsey, born May 31, 1947. Married twice: first July 20, 1968 to Richard J. Davis; second to Dennis James Hough. Two children to the first marriage and one to the second; born Austin, Texas:
      (1) Margaret Louise Davis, born May 1, 1970
      (2) Joshua Kinsey Davis, born January 20, 1973
      (3) Kathryn Alice Hough, born August 26, 1983.
   c. Ella Susan Kinsey, born July 26, 1949. Married May 9, 1981 Chester Ray Williams, Jr. and had one child:
      (1) Chester Ray Williams, III, born March 12, 1974 at Dallas, Texas.
   d. Alice Dolly Kinsey, born August 27, 1955 and married twice: first to Derry Lloyd Trice and second May 2, 1981 to James Andrew Ward. One child:
      (1) James Maxwell Ward, born December 1, 1985 at San Antonio, Texas.
3. Roy Hamilton Biser, Jr., born June 12, 1922. Married Helen Marie Osborn, born June 11, 1922. Lived in Fredericksburg, Texas and had three children:
   a. Roy Osborn Biser, born September 29, 1947. Married June 13, 1970 to Merri Gay Beatty, born in Beaumont. Roy is a minsiter of the Methodist Church, and was last reported living in Tyler, Texas.
   b. Daniel Reed Biser, born September 18, 1949 in Beaumont, Texas. Married June 26, 1976 to JoAnne

Barefoot, born January 31, 1954. He had three children, born in Whiteville, North Carolina:

(1) Julianna Blake Biser, born February 28, 1978
(2) Jonathan Blair Biser, born August 5, 1980
(3) Jennifer Marie Biser, born April 18, 1985

c. John Arthur Biser, born November 4, 1952. Married November 23, 1972 to Lisa Crittenden. They lived in Oak Park, Illinois.

4. Susan Alice Biser, born June 3, 1924 in Glasgow, Barren County, Kentucky. Married June 5, 1948 in Henrietta, Clay County, Texas, to John Thomas McCoppin, Jr. and had three children:

a. Molly Mountjoy McCoppin, born November 4, 1950. Married John Rupert Burleigh, Jr. and had three children, born in Orange County, Texas:

(1) John Rupert Burleigh, III: May 15, 1971
(2) James Christopher Burleigh: February 4, 1974
(3) Jeremy Lee Burleigh: December 12, 1977.

b. John Thomas McCoppin, III, born September 3, 1952. Married to Dorothy Lancaster and had two children:

(1) Leslie Lancaster McCoppin, born December 31, 1980
(2) Mary Elizabeth McCoppin, born August 13, 1982.

c. Emmett Ray McCoppin, born August 13, 1955. Married Angela Milam; three children, born Orange County, Texas:

(1) Emmett Ray McCoppin, Jr.: October 16, 1978
(2) Elizabeth Grace McCoppin: June 20, 1982.
(3) Emily Ann McCoppin, born August 23, 1983

David Stottlemyer
Born Germany
died c.1791
The Immigrant
*
David Stottlemyer, Jr.
died c.1821
*
Daniel Stottlemyer
1796-1864
*

*   *   *   *   *   *
*
*   * Jonathan Recher Stottlemyer
*
*   * Joseph Stottlemyer
*
*   * Rose Anna Stottlemyer 1827 .... Chapter 5
*
*   * Frederick A. Stottlemyer 1830
*
*   * Leah Ann Stottlemyer 1832
*
*   * Lydia Stottlemyer 1833
*
*   * Mary Ann Stottlemyer 1835
*
*   * Elias R. Stottlemyer 1841
*
*   * Henry F. C. Stottlemyer 1842
*
*   * Margaret Ann Rebecca Stottlemyer
*
*   * Daniel Stottlemyer, Jr.
*
*   * Cyrus Stottlemyer
*
*   * Christopher Stottlemyer

CHAPTER 4

Daniel Stottlemyer
1796-1864

This son of David Stottlemyer, Jr. (died 1821) was born September 21, 1796 on a farm northwest of Middletown, in Frederick County, and died April 21, 1874. Daniel was a minister of the Lutheran Church, stationed at Hagerstown at the time of his marriage. He is buried with his wife at the Wolfsville Reformed Church. He signed his will on January 21, 1872, and it was entered for record June 1, 1874 in Book SGC-1 at folio 486, in Frederick County, Maryland. There, he states that he is of the Catoctin District, in the county, and leaves to his wife, Johanna, all of his estate during her lifetime, and at her death, to his children in certain specific bequests. Married November 19, 1819 to Johanna Recher, born November 8, 1798, died July 5, 1895 (or June 28, 1895), at the age of 97 years, daughter of John Recher (1765) and Rosanna Protzman (1772). Johanna's paternal grandparents were Peter Recher and Mary Linebaugh, who came from Switzerland to Frederick County in the early years. The various bequests include division of his property, being several tracts of land, described as being: parts of *Yost's Claim Enlarged; Dehart's Hunting Lodge; Stone Garden; Leatherman's Luck; Yost's Lot; Timber Land; Six Daughters; Almost Night; I Will Take It All; Stoney Valley; Murdock's Inheritance; Peace Approaching, Resurvey on Almost Night;* and *Yost's Pleasant Place.* Some of the parcels include references to the lands of Daniel and Jonathan Stottlemyer as adjoining tracts. After the death of his wife, the remaining property was to be sold off and there is a specific list of bequests to the children, all named. There is also a provision that certain of his sons shall share in the usage of the saw mill yard, and water rights. Witnesses to the will were Daniel W. Bickerstaff, Joseph Stottlemyer, and Jonathan D. English. Executor was son Joseph. There were thirteen children, not necessarily in this order:

1. Jonathan Recher Stottlemyer, of whom more as Child 1.
2. Joseph Stottlemyer, probably the same who married Hannah Hauver under a license dated March 31, 1848 in Frederick County. She was a daughter of Christian Hauver (1801) and Mary Brown, of Hauver District, in Frederick County.
3. Rose Anna Stottlemyer, born 1827, of whom more in Chapter 5
4. Frederick A. Stottlemyer, born May 22, 1830, died February 6, 1913. Buried at the Wolfsville Lutheran Church in Frederick County. Married to Louisa Schildknecht in Frederick County by license dated March 24, 1856. She was born 1836 and died April 20, 1898 at age 62 years, 4 months and 11 days; buried with her husband. There is also a daughter and a son buried with their parents; could have been more:
   a. Manzella Stottlemyer, born c.1857, died March 25, 1900 at the age of 43 years, 8 months and 1 day.
   b. Francis Marion Stottlemyer, born c.1864, died March 20, 1878 at the age of 14 years, 5 months and 1 day.
5. Leah Ann Stottlemyer, born January 11, 1832, of whom more as Child 5, following.
6. Lydia Stottlemyer, born August 5, 1833, died July 30, 1905. Marriage certificate taken in Frederick County, November 9, 1854 to William Hauver, born 1831, died June 7, 1889 at the age of 58 years, 7 months and 9 days. Buried at Wolfsville Reformed Church. Children, including at least these:
   a. Ida T. Hauver, born May 23, 1858 at Foxville, Frederick County, Maryland. Married Wilson L. Pryor,

born July 15, 1854 on the family farm about one mile north of Foxville, Maryland, son of Samuel H. Pryor and Dorothy Wolf. Wilson owned several farms, finally settling near Thurmont, Maryland on a farm he purchased from Henry Sipes. Two children, one being:

(1) William S. Pryor.

b. An infant, died January 14, 1873 buried with parents

7. Mary Ann Stottlemyer, born April 12, 1835, died March 10, 1887. Married March 1, 1866 at Wolfsville, Maryland, to William Warren Troxell, born January 14, 1841 near Thurmont, in Frederick County, son of David Troxell (1806) and Juliann Feiser (1809). They had at least these children, born in Frederick County, Maryland:

a. Henry David Troxell, born November 18, 1866, died June 14, 1927 at Medford, Oregon. Married to Elva Janette Young, born February 12, 1868, died May 3, 1948 at Tingley, Idaho. Children, born Maryland:

(1) Earl Bryon Troxell, born April 17, 1897, died 1973 in Tingley, Idaho.

(2) Wayne Nebraska Troxell, born March 28, 1899

(3) Lloyd Ervin Troxell, born November 19, 1903 and died 1904

b. Lewis Edward Troxell, born c.1868

c. Joseph Recker Troxell, born August 26, 1870, died April 6, 1891.

d. Jasper Newton Troxell, born June 20, 1872, died c.1935 at Paris, Missouri.

e. Roy Emanuel Troxell, born April 4, 1874, died 1907

f. Ida K. Troxell, born July 17, 1875

g. Gertrude Troxell, born October 25, 1877, died July 12, 1930

8. Elias R. Stottlemyer, born c.1841; reportedly the Elias R. married October 22, 1863 to Eliza Victoria Hauver in

Frederick County. She was born December 1, 1842, died April 4, 1871 at age 28 years, 4 months, 3 days; buried Wolfsville Brethren Church; daughter of Gideon Hauver and Elizabeth Remsberg. They had children, born at Wolfsville, Frederick County, Maryland:

a. Etta May Stottlemyer, born c.1865
b. Carrie Teresa Stottlemyer, born February 25, 1867 and died December 29, 1958
c. Dewitt Clinton Stottlemyer, born June 5, 1869, died June 16, 1890; buried with his mother.

9. Henry F. C. Stottlemyer, born 1842, of whom more
10. Margaret Ann Rebecca Stottlemyer; marriage license dated April 27, 1864 to Lawson Palmer in Frederick County.
11. Daniel Stottlemyer, Jr.
12. Cyrus Stottlemyer.
13. Christopher Stottlemyer.

CHILD 1

Jonathan Recher Stottlemyer
c.1823-

This son of Daniel Stottlemyer (1796) and Johanna Recher (1798) appears on a marriage license dated November 5, 1842 to Susanna Blickenstaff, at Middletown, in Frederick County. She was born July 9, 1823 and died February 10, 1893, daughter of John Blickenstaff and Mary Fair. We can perhaps safely assume that Jonathan was born c.1823 as well. They had children:

1. Ruth Ann Lavina Stottlemyer.
2. Mary Elenore Stottlemyer.
3. Flavous Josephus Stottlemyer. This individual was found in Mormon Church records as Joseph, born about 1847 in Washington County, Maryland. He was married there

to Mary Venelia Dutrow, born there May 22, 1851, daughter of Leonard Dutrow and Amelie Horlie. They had children, born Washington County:

a. Asa Paul Stottlemyer.
b. Agatna, perhaps actually Agatha Stottlemyer.
c. Claine Stottlemyer.
d. Jonathan Leonard Stottlemyer, born 1892, died 1971. Married Phebe Alice Miller, born October 5, 1895, daughter of Otho James Miller (1856) and Florence Estelle Biser (1858) of Boonesboro. They had children:
    (1) Philip Rene Stottlemyer, born November 28, 1932. Married Evelyn, and had children:
        (a) Mark Allan Stottlemyer, married Rhoda Smith and had a son:
            1. Troy Tyler Stottlemyer, born August 15, 1987
        (b) Lisa Marie Stottlemyer.
        (c) Kathy Ann Stottlemyer.
    (2) Jean Carol Stottlemyer, born April 9, 1934. Married to Arnold Gustav Swenson, born April 30, 1934. Children:
        (a) Timothy Conrad Swenson, born June 5, 1956. Married Janice Kooiman and had children:
            1. Mathew Swenson.
            2. Paul Swenson.
        (b) Gary Arnold Swenson, born September 30, 1960
        (c) Carol Alice Swenson: December 8, 1964
        (d) Daniel Hjalmer Swenson, born November 10, 1975.
    (3) Margaret Ann Stottlemyer, born June 14, 1936. Married Swisher; lives in Florida.

CHILD 5

Leah Ann Stottlemyer
1832-

This daughter of Daniel Stottlemyer (1796) and Johanna Recher (1798) was born January 11, 1832. Married to Silas Buhrman, born 1828 on the family homestead in Hauvers District of Frederick County. He died October 10, 1892 and is buried at Mount Bethel Church. He was a son of Henry Buhrman, Jr. and Ann Barnes. Silas was a land assessor in Frederick County, and a member of the board of County School Commissioners. Ten of their eleven children reached maturity:

1. Manzella Buhrman, married to E. M. Z. Buhrman, her second cousin.
2. Sida H. Buhrman, born September 11, 1854, died 1941; buried at Mt. Bethel Methodist Church. He purchased a farm from his father about one mile south of Foxville, in Frederick County, where he made his home. He was postmaster under President Harrison, and a census enumerator in 1900. Married to Mary J. Buhrman, who was not a relative, born 1854 and died March 6, 1886, daughter of David Buhrman and Hannah Pryor. Five years after her death, Sida H. Buhrman was married second to Jane E., the widow of Henry Hoffman. Two children were born to his first marriage; none to the second:
    a. Elsie I. Buhrman, married to Harley Sipe, an electrician; lived in Lima, Ohio.
    b. Harry S. Buhrman.
3. Elias M. Buhrman, who moved to California.
4. Emory L. Buhrman, lived in Washington County, Maryland.
5. Kate A. Buhrman.
6. Harvey M. Buhrman, a rural mail carrier.

7. Minnie M. Buhrman, lived in Hagerstown.
8. Addie C. Buhrman, married her distant cousin, Albert L. Buhrman. These are perhaps the same two of these names who are buried at Thurmont United Baptist Church; she is there called Ada C., born 1869, and died 1946. He is Albert L., born 1855, died 1929.
9. Alfred R. Buhrman, who was a dealer in produce in Catoctin District.
10. Vernon M. Buhrman.

CHILD 9

Henry F. C. Stottlemyer
1842-

This son of Daniel Stottlemyer (1796) was born April 22, 1842 on the old homestead about one mile northeast of Wolfsville, in Frederick County, Maryland. He remained on the family farm until the death of his father, when he inherited part of the lands in his own name. Upon that property, he remodeled the old dwelling, and added a second story; erected a barn and all other necessary outbuildings. He was married to Martha E. Brown, daughter of William B. Brown and Elizabeth Fox, and had at least four children:

1. Worth B. Stottlemyer, born April 11, 1875, died November 11, 1951; buried at Wolfsville Reformed cemetery. He became a teller in the Bank of Waynesboro, Pennsylvania; and Treasurer of the Chambersburg, Greencastle and Waynesboro Street Railway Company.
2. Claud U. Stottlemyer, who became General Manager for the Geiser Manufacturing Co. of Louisville, Kentucky.
3. Olga D. Stottlemyer.
4. Irma M. Stottlemyer.

David Stottlemyer
Born Germany
died c.1791
The Immigrant
*
*
David Stottlemyer, Jr.
died c.1821
*
*
Daniel Stottlemyer
1796-1864
*
*
Rose Anna Stottlemyer
1827-
*
*

*   *   *   *   *   *
*
*   * Melvin Americus Emerenth Biser 1853
*
*   * Thaddeus McAuley Biser 1854
*
*   * Lillie May Biser 1856
*
*   * Florence E. Biser
*
*   * Emma R. Biser
*
*   * Ruth A. Biser
*
*   * Cyrus Carty Biser
*
*   * Irving S. Biser 1869
*
*   * Victor R. S. Biser

CHAPTER 5

Rose Anna Stottlemyer
1827-1911

This daughter of Daniel Stottlemyer (1796) and Johanna Recher (1798), was born March 10, 1827 in Frederick County, Maryland, and died May 18, 1911. Various records show her name as Roseanna or Rose Ann, but this appears to be the correct spelling. She was married in the county by license dated December 16, 1851 to Daniel A. Biser, born August 10, 1828 in the Jackson District of Frederick County, died August 20, 1899, son of Jacob Biser and Catherine Brandenburg. The couple are buried at the Reformed Church cemetery in Wolfsville, where they were active all their lives. Daniel A. Biser was an elected commissioner for Frederick County for two years beginning 1875. The Black Rock Road, connecting Frederick and Washington Counties across South Mountain, was built during his administration. He was a farmer and a miller in the Catoctin and Jackson Districts of the county, where they lived their entire lives, and raised their rather large family. His grist mill was located on the Middlepoint Road, and was locally known as the Duvall Mill, the person from whom Daniel purchased it. They had nine children, eight of whom survived to adult ages:

1. Melvin Americus Emerenth Biser, born January 23, 1853, of whom more as Child 1, following.
2. Thaddeus McCauley Biser, born October 22, 1854 and of whom more as Child 2.
3. Lillie May Biser, born September 10, 1856, died May 30, 1858. Buried Myersville Lutheran church cemetery.
4. Florence Estelle Biser, born October 19, 1858, of whom more as Child 4.

5. Emma Reno Biser, born June 16, 1862, of whom more as Child 5.
6. Ruth Ann Cecilia Biser, born May 17, 1864, of whom more as Child 6.
7. Cyrus Carty Biser, born May 6, 1866, died December 24, 1951; single. He was a teacher in Frederick County and is buried in the Rest Haven Cemetery, Hagerstown.
8. Irving Stanton Biser, born January 10, 1869, and died March, 1951. He worked for the Post Office after thirteen years as a teacher, including several years as Assistant Principal of the Frederick High School. He was a talented musician, leading the Braddock band and orchestra for twelve years. Married June 26, 1894 Celeste Grace Stone, born 1876, died October 4, 1947, daughter of Joseph D. Stone and Harriet E. McDevitt. One daughter:
    a. Lillian Barrett Biser, born 1896, died of kidney disease in 1913.
9. Victor Recher Santee Biser, born August 9, 1871, and of whom more as Child 9.

CHILD 1

Melvin Americus Emerenth Biser
1853-1915

This son of Daniel A. Biser (1828) and Rose Anna Stottlemyer (1827) was born January 23, 1853, and died March 25, 1915. He was a teacher in Frederick County schools from 1875 to 1897. He and Charles J. Stottlemyer were publishers of *The Catoctin News* from 1887 to 1892, when he sold his interests. In 1897, he was appointed Deputy Clerk of the Circuit Court for a term of six years. In 1903 he was appointed the Deputy Register of Wills for six years. Married twice: first in December, 1878 to Marietta M. Hayes, daughter of

John Otto Hayes and Sophia Fox. She died June 25, 1887, having had three children. He was married second 1891 to Esta Mae Neikirk from Middletown, and had seven children, for a total of eleven from his two marriages:

1. Rosa S. Biser, died March 16, 1887
2. Pearl Harp Biser, born April 13, 1880, died July 6, 1905. Married Henry Glaze Huffer, born c.1877, died March 16, 1911 at age 34 years 5 months and 25 days. Both buried at Mt. Olivet cemetery, Frederick They had four children, only one of whom survived to adulthood:
   a. Robert Huffer, died July 3, 1903
   b. Josephine Huffer, died September 22, 1904
   c. Roger Huffer, died August 19, 1905
   d. Naomi Margaret Huffer, born September 14, 1903, died August 7, 1981. Married November 3, 1951 to Theodore Roosevelt Ables, born August 29, 1907, died April, 1980.
3. Erie Calvin Biser, born September 16, 1882, and of whom more following.
4. Mary Magdalene Biser, of whom more following.
5. Irma Rae Biser, born February 10, 1896, of whom more following.
6. Frank Masta Biser, born August 17, 1900, and died March 30, 1973. He served in the first world war and settled in Cortland, Ohio, where he was married. After the death of his wife, he returned to Frederick; no children were reported.
7. Irving Melvin Biser, born May 19, 1905, died April 13, 1984. Married Virginia L. Stewart; two children:
   a. Doris Virginia Biser, born April 16, 1932. Married Ralph Mills and divorced; one son:
      (1) David W. Mills.
   b. Betty Leona Biser, born January 4, 1934. Married to Bayard Rosencrantz, born September 19, 1926, died November 27, 1981. Three children:

(1) Sarah Virginia Rosencrantz, born September 2, 1959. Married Joseph F. Wills.
(2) Faith Lee Rosencrantz: October 25, 1961
(3) Bayard Rosencrantz, Jr: January 16, 1965

8. George Wier Biser, married Helen Kefauver and was divorced after three children:
   a. Gary R. Biser, born April 10, 1941
   b. Robert L. Biser, born March 27, 1944
   c. Anita L. Biser, born April 20, 1945
9. May Biser, born February, 1894, and died March 1, 1897
10. Amy Biser, born July, 1898, died April 18, 1899

Erie Calvin Biser
1882-1957

This son of Melvin Americus Emerenth Biser (1853) was born September 16, 1882, and died June 26, 1957. Married October 5, 1912 to Lizzie Adeline Coblentz, born October 3, 1888, died March 6, 1979. They are buried in the Middletown Reformed Church cemetery. They lived on a farm in the Adamstown area, and had eleven children:

1. Richard Calvin Biser, born July 15, 1913, died March 4, 1980. Married April 13, 1940 Emma Susan Geisler, born January 25, 1919. Four children:
   a. Richard Calvin Biser, Jr., born December 30, 1941. Married August 30, 1969 to Julia Jeanne Culler, born March 17, 1943. One daughter:
      (1) Susan Julia Biser, born May 28, 1971
   b. Joan Celeste Biser: September 12, 1944.
   c. Martha Carole Biser, born April 9, 1949. Married October 18, 1969 to William Patrick Kokosko, born March 17, 1949. Two children:
      (1) Angela Lynn Kokosko, born August 18, 1970
      (2) Tricia Lea Kokosko, born May 13, 1975.

d. Darla Jeanne Biser, born January 24, 1953. Married twice: first February 10, 1973 to Elbert Sanders Cheeks; divorced. Married second August 7, 1982 to Wade B. Clem, born May 25, 1957. One child:
   (1) Tara Jeanne Cheeks, born July 22, 1973

2. Frances Elizabeth Biser, born April 25, 1915, died October 11, 1974. Married Karl Wilhelm Henn, born May 29, 1905, died March 6, 1983. Buried at Middletown Reformed Church cemetery, Frederick County, Maryland. Two children:
   a. Karl Martin Henn, born April 12, 1937. Married June 20, 1971 to Joyce Marilyn McCarty, born August 26, 1945. Two children:
      (1) Karl William Henn, born November 10, 1975
      (2) Matt Herman Henn, born February 11, 1978
   b. Ellen Frances Henn, born October 31, 1941. Married December 30, 1961 to James Douglas Murray, born August 14, 1940. Two children:
      (1) Colleen Marie Murray, born October 11, 1962
      (2) Kathleen Ellen Murray, born December 5, 1964. Married December 29, 1986 to George Kopcsak.

3. Margaret Coblentz Biser, born June 9, 1916. Married September 18, 1935 to Albert Melvin Ringer, born March 10, 1913. Two children:
   a. Judith Adaline Ringer, born July 26, 1942. Married June 9, 1962 to Wayne Eugene Ott, born May 28, 1941. Three children:
      (1) Adalyn Diane Ott, born January 22, 1964. Married November 6, 1982 Scott Jason Wanrow, born February 29, 1964. Two children:
         (a) Timothy Wanrow.
         (b) Jason Wanrow.
      (2) Timothy Wayne Ott, born May 30, 1966.
      (3) Jason Richard Ott, born May 30, 1970

b. Melvin Erie Ringer, born September 12, 1943. Married April 2, 1966 to Theresa Mary Clancy, born April 12, 1945. Two children:
   (1) Troy Erie Ringer, born October 19, 1969
   (2) Mary Margaret Ringer, born Mary 18, 1972

4. Helen Biser, born September 9, 1917. Married December 24, 1949 to Grayson Palmer Snook, born May 17, 1909, died September 5, 1970. One son, adopted:
   a. Dennis Irvin Snook, born February 16, 1950. Married twice: first May 11, 1971 to Shyra Jane Hahn, born September 21, 1950, divorced. Married second May 24, 1984 to Connie Duggan, born October 24, 1955. Two children:
      (1) Nikki Michele Snook, born April 24, 1973
      (2) Natalie Jane Snook, born August 5, 1975

5. Marietta Biser, born September 16, 1919. Married December 6, 1938 to Charles Franklin Lewis, born March 6, 1918. Three children:
   a. Charles Edwin Lewis, born August 16, 1941. Married first January 23, 1965 to Diane Brightwell, born January 11, 1946 and divorced. Two children:
      (1) Denis Wayne Lewis, born May 25, 1966
      (2) Chad Eugene Lewis, born April 14, 1969
   b. Donald Eugene Lewis, born December 9, 1947. Married June 20, 1970 to Nancy Darlene Wickline, born March 24, 1948. Two children:
      (1) Karen Adell Lewis, born October 25, 1981
      (2) Todd Everett Lewis, born March 9, 1984
   c. Neil Eric Lewis, born November 4, 1952. Married January 4, 1986 to Lynn Vogel, born July 26, 1956. One child reported:
      (1) Danielle Shea Lewis, born September 1, 1986

6. Joseph Erie Biser, born December 23, 1920. Married April 2, 1942 to Mary Alice Mercer, born January 8, 1924. Four children:

a. Joseph Erie Biser, Jr., born February 15, 1944. Married March 17, 1979 to Ruth Moncure, and had two children:
   (1) Joseph Thomas Biser, born July 1, 1979
   (2) Jennifer Lorraine Biser: February 17, 1982
b. Robert Coblentz Biser, born June 18, 1946. Married October 12, 1969 to Christine Jane Easton, born October 18, 1948. One adopted child:
   (1) Mandy Joe Biser, born December 21, 1976
c. Daniel Calvin Biser, born December 20, 1947. Married December 27, 1973 to Sarah Middleton Heslep, born October 5, 1954. Three children:
   (1) Daniel William Biser, born July 12, 1978
   (2) Abby Marie Biser, born July 14, 1979
   (3) Dale Ezra Biser, born August 1, 1980
d. Brenda Joyce Biser, born February 20, 1949. Married twice: first August 31, 1968 to Richard Stone, born August 10, 1947, died May 30, 1969. Married second December 27, 1969 to Craig Rhoderick, born April 23, 1947, divorced. One child:
   (1) Kyle Aaron Rhoderick: December 9, 1970

7. Paul Melvin Biser, born June 12, 1922. Married June 17, 1948 to Margaret B. Munday, born June 14, 1928. Two children:
   a. Paula Sue Biser, born February 24, 1949. Married October 5, 1985 to Gary Wayne Tomey.
   b. Gary Melvin Biser, born February 27, 1953. Married March 17, 1972 to Brenda Jean Wiles, born March 28, 1954. Two children:
      (1) Scott Allan Biser, born March 11, 1972
      (2) Brian Melvin Biser, born August 2, 1976
8. Martin Roland Biser, born August 25, 1923. Married July 11, 1947 to Evelyn Lorraine Stup, born December 1, 1926. Two children:

a. Gale Lorraine Biser, born January 14, 1953. Married August 4, 1973 to Robert Lee Grams, Jr., born February 2, 1954. Two children:
   (1) Jennifer Lynne Grams, born April 19, 1978
   (2) Rick Michael Grams, born April 8, 1980
b. Linda Kay Biser, born November 26, 1964. Married December 8, 1973 to Thomas Owens Murray, Jr., born June 7, 1950. Two children:
   (1) Brad Alan Murray, born August 7, 1976
   (2) Jeffery Wayne Murray, born June 18, 1978

9. Dorothy Ellen Biser, born August 14, 1925. Married first October 9, 1944 to Harry L. Southerly, born April 3, 1936 and died February 2, 1976. They were divorced and she married second May 2, 1966 to Chester E. Libby born January 28, 1920. Two children:
   a. Olivia Lee Southerly, born October 8, 1948. Married August 20, 1966 to Palmer E. Mays, born November 4, 1946; divorced after one child:
      (1) Christopher Lee Mays, born March 19, 1967
   b. Laney Calvin Southerly, born October 12, 1961

10. Katharine Beatrice Biser, born January 10, 1927. Married June 23, 1945 to James E. Houff, born May 14, 1924, and had two children:
   a. Edward Francis Houff, born April 8, 1946. Married August 31, 1968 to Catherine Adeline Kane, born May 3, 1947. Two children:
      (1) Alexandra Marie Houff, born July 15, 1972
      (2) Abigail Lynn Houff, born February 13, 1979
   b. Jennifer Louise Houff, born July 27, 1948. Married April 26, 1969 to Charles E. Bradley, Jr., born August 16, 1946. Two children:
      (1) Sarah Paige Bradley, born October 9, 1978
      (2) Ian Mechener Bradley, born July 14, 1983

11. Julia Lorraine Biser, born March 5, 1930. Married June 23, 1949 to James Thomas Duncan, born March 14, 1924. Two children:
    a. Lynn Dianne Duncan, born November 21, 1952. Married first September 11, 1976 to Christopher D. Wilson and divorced. Married second 1984 Charles Hammons. One child:
        (1) Duncan Gregory Hammons, born July 4, 1985
    b. Jan Lorraine Duncan, born July 5, 1955. Married September 3, 1977 to Charles Fielder Goddard, born November 14, 1952. Two children:
        (1) Charles Fielder Goddard, Jr.: March 19, 1981
        (2) Rachael Lorraine Goddard: June 7, 1983

Mary Magdalene Biser
1892-1966

This daughter of Melvin Americus Emerenth Biser (1853) was born March 8, 1892, died December 17, 1966. Married June 3, 1919 to Jesse Melvin Knill, born May 22, 1893, died April 2, 1950 and had two children:

1. Margaret Louise Knill. Married February 12, 1944 to Francis Faust Seidel, II, born August 23, 1916. One son, born in Pennsylvania:
    a. Francis Faust Seidel, III, born December 15, 1956. Married October 13, 1974 to Wanda Lee Michael, born October 15, 1947. One son:
        (1) Francis Faust Seidel, IV, born April 18, 1978
2. Mary Jane Knill. Married January 26, 1946 to Richard H. Cliff, Jr., born August 29, 1920. Two children:
    a. Nancy Jane Cliff, born January 15, 1947. She married June 24, 1967 to Najatolla Younessi, born June 4, 1942. Two sons:
        (1) Theodore A. Younessi: October 30, 1970
        (2) Timothy Younessi: July 15, 1977

b. Mary Ann Cliff, born August 5, 1948. Married Kenneth Sperow, born April 3, 1938. A daughter:
   (1) Richelle Sperow: March 31, 1978

Irma Rae Biser
1896-1966

This daughter of Melvin Americus Emerenth Biser (1853) was born February 10, 1896, died July 31, 1966. Married March 5, 1918 to David Emanuel Zimmerman, born October 20, 1885, died January 25, 1963. Five children:

1. Elizabeth Zimmerman, born August 11, 1919. Married January 27, 194? to John Griffith Woodfield, born February 23, 1912, died March 17, 1984. Three children:
   a. Margaret Elizabeth Woodfield, born November 30, 1940, died February 25, 1959.
   b. Joanne Louise Woodfield, born August 17, 1947. Married July 10, 1965 to Thomas L. Wetherell and had three children:
      (1) Christine Elaine Wetherell: August 27, 1967
      (2) John Thomas Wetherell: April 11, 1969
      (3) Daniel Lee Wetherell: June 18, 1970
   c. James Griffith Woodfield, born August 10, 1954
2. Charles Howard Zimmerman, born September 8, 1922. Married May 5, 1945 to Mildred Irene Smith, born May 31, 1920. They had a foster son:
   a. George Clayton Stevens. Married July 12, 1959 to Larue Helen Summers, born July 28, 1941. They had two children:
      (1) Robert Clayton Stevens, born January 12, 1960. Married July 20, 1982 to Diane Yvonne Cole. One child:
         (a) Heather Nicole Stevens.
      (2) Patricia Marie Stevens, married Burdette and had a child:

(a) Steven Cole Burdette.

3. Melvin Americath Zimmerman, born August 13, 1925. Married June 4, 1950 to Kathleen Estelle Page, born May 12, 1929. Four children:
   a. Victoria Ruth Zimmerman, born May 23, 1954
   b. Carolyn Page Zimmerman, born October 1, 1958
   c. Charles David Zimmerman, born January 24, 1964
   d. Russell Charles Oden, born June 26, 1947, a foster son. Married Susan Albina Buchanan, born April 5, 1947. Three children:
      (1) Constance Lynn Oden, born October 21, 1967
      (2) Russell Jacob Oden, born October 19, 1971
      (3) Pamela Sue Oden, born March 15, 1973
4. Irma Rae Zimmerman, born June 28, 1930. Married September 29, 1951 to George William Anderson, born August 7, 1928. Four children:
   a. George William Anderson, Jr., born January 14, 1953. Married May 14, 1977 to Patricia Bogart.
   b. Gina Marie Anderson, born December 8, 1954. Married first June 10, 1972 to Darius Levi Ecker and divorced. Married second October 28, 1983 to Gerald Gigeous. One daughter and two stepsons:
      (1) Christie Ann Ecker.
      (2) James Gigeous.
      (3) Robert Gigeous.
   c. Gregg Michael Anderson, born September 30, 1962. Married October 19, 1985 to Doreen Hess.
   d. Glenn Robert Anderson, born August 26, 1966.
5. David Emanuel Zimmerman, born August 30, 1934. Married May 24, 1953 to Doris Geraldine Bowers, born October 6, 1933. Six children:
   a. Jane Marie Zimmerman, twin, born October 16, 1953, and married December 10, 1983 to Richard Younkins.

b. Janet Louise Zimmerman, twin, born October 16, 1953.
c. David Douglas Zimmerman, born October 28, 1954. Married April 19, 1980 to Mary Virginia Humbert, born November 2, 1957.
d. Marvin Wayne Zimmerman, born July 28, 1957. Married March 19, 1983 to Dorothy Marie Moser, born March 1, 1953.
e. Austin Leroy Zimmerman, born April 15, 1960 and married August 8, 1981 to Dolores Ann Sylvain, born June 12, 1959.
f. Faye Lorraine Zimmerman, born May 29, 1961 and married to Freeman H. Wagoner, Jr., born September 14, 1957.

CHILD 2

Thaddeus McCauley Biser
1854-

This son of Daniel A. Biser (1828) and Rose Anna Stottlemyer (1827) was born October 22, 1854 at Wolfsville, and died of cancer September 18, 1910. He became an attorney and practiced in Frederick County. In the 1880 census, he was living in a boarding house, and listed as a professor, teaching school, and director of a band. Married December 31, 1889 to Jennie Irene Thomas, born April 22, 1867, died July 29, 1936, daughter of Zacharias Thomas and Louisa Grove. In 1906, he built the home locally known as *Sandigan* on the Shookstown Road out of Frederick, which has since been demolished. Nine children:

1. Nevin McCauley Biser, born August 8, 1890, died August 19, 1977. Married Bertha Howe Habenicht, born February 12, 1895, died April 21, 1979. They had five children:

a. Margaret Amelia Biser, born May 28, 1919. Married Lowell Myers Watkins, born October 19, 1922. He was a music teacher at James Madison University in Harrisonburg, Virginia, and they had three children:
   (1) Jean Yvonne Watkins: August 27, 1952
   (2) Christopher Lowell Watkins, born November 20, 1953
   (3) Barbara Louise Watkins, born May 26, 1955. Married Jeffrey Stuart Reech, born January 25, 1953. One child:
      (a) Christopher Stuart Reech, born February 27, 1983.

b. Jean Yvonne Watkins, born June 13, 1921. Married James Tolliver Wortham from Columbia, South Carolina, born September 10, 1924, died February 2, 1960. Three children:
   (1) Martha Douglass Wortham, born June 22, 1951. Married Thomas Nathaniel Fowler, Jr., born April 13, 1951. Two children:
      (a) Kathleen Allison Fowler, born August 15, 1980
      (b) Thomas Nathaniel Fowler, III, born June 7, 1983.
   (2) Mary Margaret Wortham, born March 25, 1956; married William Christopher Brown born December 28, 1953.
   (3) James Tolliver Wortham, Jr., born February 3, 1959

c. Hubert Habenicht Biser, born April 30, 1924. Married Mildred Schalkhauser, born November 11, 1922, of Ohio. Lived in Orangeburg, South Carolina; five children:
   (1) Mark Hubert Biser, born October 11, 1951. Married Elizabeth Olrogg, born July 30, 1952.

(2) Lynn Biser, born June 28, 1953. Married Arthur Emerson Brantley, born March 10, 1949. Two children:
   (a) Benjamin David Brantley born March 24, 1979
   (b) Jessica Lauren Brantley, born May 30, 1982.
(3) Janet Biser, born July 28, 1954. Married Kirk Perry Bridgers, born April 11, 1952. One child:
   (a) John Kirk Bridgers: April 15, 1980
(4) David Frederick Biser, born August 19, 1958. Married Jamie Gerry, born June 26, 1954. Four children:
   (a) Snannon Angela Biser: April 29, 1973
   (b) Adrienne Mae Biser: March 5, 1978
   (c) Justin David Biser: September 3, 1983
   (d) Kasie Marie Biser: August 6, 1984
(5) Joan Biser, born January 2, 1961. Married Karl Frederick Suhr, born April 1, 1957.

d. Nevin McCauley Biser, Jr., born July 20, 1926 and married Sarah Bedell, born March 30, 1928. Lived in Lexington, South Carolina; two children:
(1) Donna Marie Biser, born June 2, 1958
(2) Patricia Ann Biser, born September 15, 1959. Married to Nunnamaker.

e. Christopher Habenicht Biser, born October 4, 1929. He is a doctor of radiology in Columbia, South Carolina. Married to Mary Elizabeth Conolly, born November 25, 1956, and had five children:
(1) DeAnne Biser, born December, 1960
(2) Carlyn Biser, born April, 1963
(3) Thaddeus Habenicht Biser, born 1972
(4) Robin Ann Biser, born 1974

(5) Christopher Habenicht Biser, Jr., born February 3, 1978

2. Sherwood Thomas Biser, born January 12, 1893, died November 21, 1898.
3. Eloise Biser, born September 15, 1894. Married Thomas Russell Sheehy, who died in 1970. Two children:
   a. Thomas Russell Sheehy, Jr., born July 9, 1922 and died during the second world war.
   b. Frederick Biser Sheehy, born September 1, 1925
4. Rosabelle Biser, born October 11, 1896. Married Homer Lee McCormick, born August 3, 1897 from Oklahoma, died April 24, 1968. They had four children, who lived in California:
   a. Homer Lee McCormick, Jr.
   b. Patricia McCormick, married Baer.
   c. William McCormick.
   d. Peter McCormick.
5. Thaddeus McCauley Biser, Jr., born January 15, 1902, died January, 1985. Married September 22, 1934 to Helen Beusing, born October 18, 1911. Two children:
   a. Marie Elaine Biser, born October 14, 1938. Married December 15, 1957 to John M. Gordon, and had two children:
      (1) Elizabeth Ann Gordon: September 18, 1958
      (2) Bruce Vrommer Gordon: October 4, 1961
   b. Margaret Elizabeth Biser, born April 5, 1946. Married May 13, 1972 William Streeter. Two children:
      (1) Jonathan Neil Streeter: June 17, 1979
      (2) Kira Elizabeth Streeter: October 10, 1982
6. Mildred Biser, born January 4, 1900, died August 9, 1983. Married to C. Lawrence Smith and divorced, with no children. She was a graduate of Johns Hopkins School of Nursing in 1925, and followed a successful career in that field, founding the Glenmerrie Nursing Home

at Point of Rocks, Maryland, which she operated until her retirement in 1964.

7. Yvonne Biser, born August 6, 1905, died March 22, 1980. Married Daniel Gordon, and lived in California. She graduated from Hood College in Frederick; received a Masters degree from the Peabody Conservatory in Baltimore, and taught music for a number of years. No children reported.
8. Jennie Helen Biser, born 1908, an infant death.
9. Reginald Algernon Biser, born March 1, 1910. Married Alma Arnball from Pennsylvania, born April 27, 1909. They have two adopted children:
    a. Sharyn Biser, born May 2, 1943. Married first Thad Grace and divorced. Married second to Robert Beckley, born May, 1942. Two children:
        (1) Cathryne Victoria Grace: January 30, 1964
        (2) John Craig Beckley: January 26, 1971
    b. Alan Keith Biser, born June 2, 1946. Married to Caroline Sue Morris, born September 5, 1948. Two children:
        (1) Joshua Alan Biser: October 27, 1968
        (2) Shannon Kimberly Biser: March 21, 1972

CHILD 4

Florence Estelle Biser
1858-1931

This daughter of Daniel A. Biser (1828) and Rose Anna Stottlemyer (1827) was born October 19, 1858 died August 21, 1931. Married February 27, 1888 to Otho James Miller of Boonesboro, born 1856, died 1920, son of John S. Miller (1830) and Mary A. Snyder. The farm they lived on where his father lived before him, remained in the family through the next two generations. Otho and Florence are buried in Boonesboro; six children:

1. Clarence Olin Miller, born December 29, 1888 and died August 26, 1956. Married Bess Geltmacher, born February 27, 1893, died August 16, 1964. They are buried at Boonsboro and had son son:
    a. Carroll Ivan Miller, born November 28, 1916. Married Margaret Poffenberger, born November 2, 1931. Five children:
        (1) Sharon Ann Miller, born September 7, 1949. Married Wayne Albert, and had two children:
            (a) Kimberly Albert: February 14, 1968
            (b) Kristin Albert: August 6, 1971
        (2) Larry Carroll Miller, born November 19, 1950. Married Carol Sharer, and had three children:
            (a) David Woodrow Miller, born November 11, 1975
            (b) Jason Carroll Miller: June 23, 1979
            (c) Lauri Rene Miller, born December 18, 1982
        (3) Gary Lee Miller, born February 28, 1958. Married Deborah Kline; one stepchild:
            (a) Jeremy Fiegley, born July 17, 1978
        (4) Darrin Allen Miller, born March 29, 1969
        (5) Donna Mary Miller, born May 10, 1972
3. Ruth Orpha Miller, born 1890, died 1936, single.
4. John Miller, born 1892, died 1901.
5. Rose Kathryn Miller, born October 19, 1893, died January 31, 1982. Married in 1922 as his second wife to the Reverend Harry Kottler, born September 5, 1886, died September 10, 1966. He had one child from his first marriage and three with Rose:
    a. Ferne Kottler, born January 26, 1915

b. Janet Louise Kottler, born October 10, 1924. Married Joseph Ray Arnold, born July 22, 1924 and had two children:
   (1) Janet Carol Arnold, born October 10, 1924. Married Douglas Warner and had one child:
      (a) Justin Micah Warner: February 11, 1984
   (2) Joseph Ray Arnold, Jr.: April 3, 1955
c. Frances RoseAnna Kottler, born November 26, 1927. She is a teacher, and single.
d. Patricia Lee Kottler, born December 25, 1934. Married Carl E. Morris, born July 9, 1934 and had three children:
   (1) Melissa Lee Morris: November 13, 1962
   (2) Christopher Michael Morris: October 1, 1966
   (3) Stephen Patrick Morris: September 1, 1969

6. Phebe Alice Miller, born October 5, 1895. Married to Jonathan Leonard Stottlemyer, born 1892, died 1971, son of Flavous Josephus Stottlemyer (1847) and Mary Venelia Dutrow (1851). Three children:
a. Philip Rene Stottlemyer, born November 28, 1932. Married Evelyn, and had children:
   (1) Mark Allan Stottlemyer, married Rhoda Smith and had a son:
      (a) Troy Tyler Stottlemyer: August 15, 1987
   (2) Lisa Marie Stottlemyer.
   (3) Kathy Ann Stottlemyer.
b. Jean Carol Stottlemyer, born April 9, 1934. Married to Arnold Gustav Swenson, born April 30, 1934. Children:
   (1) Timothy Conrad Swenson, born June 5, 1956. Married Janice Kooiman and had children:
      (a) Mathew Swenson.
      (b) Paul Swenson.
   (2) Gary Arnold Swenson: September 30, 1960
   (3) Carol Alice Swenson: December 8, 1964

(4) Daniel Hjalmer Swenson: November 10, 1975.

c. Margaret Ann Stottlemyer, born June 14, 1936. Married Swisher; lives in Florida.

7. Leo Daniel Miller, born c.1897. Married Winifred Gillam; no children. He was a graduate of Johns Hopkins University, and a chemist with the Musselman Company for a period of time.

CHILD 5

Emma Reno Biser
1862-1932

This daughter of Daniel A. Biser (1828) and Rose Anna Stottlemyer (1827) was born June 16, 1862, died January 6, 1932. Married October 21, 1885 to Charles Levin Grove, born October 3, 1860, died September 25, 1953, the son of James Aaron Grove and Harriet Hayes. Emma and Charles were both raised near Wolfsville, and both were teachers, as well as owners of a fruit farm. They are buried at Boonsboro. Seven children, born in Frederick Couny, Maryland:

1. Mary Rose Grove, born November 25, 1887, died June 11, 1967; buried Boonsboro. Married April 6, 1916 to Raymond E. Shifler, and had one child:
   a. Raymond E. Shifler, Jr., born February 25, 1917.
2. Emma Reno Grove, born September 21, 1889, died February 5, 1952, single; buried at Boonsboro.
3. Paul Charles Grove, born June 4, 1892, died January 1, 1978. Married June 10, 1914 to Hazel Irene Wolverton, born October 3, 1897, died March 14, 1985, daughter of Edward Wolverton and Pearl Barr of Dayton, Ohio. As a young man, Paul had moved to Springfield, Ohio, and after several moves back and forth, finally settled at Hagerstown, Washington County, Maryland. They had four children:

a. Virginia Irene Grove, born June 27, 1917. Married June 26, 1939 to Edward Leroy Baker, born October 3, 1917. No children.
b. Pauline Victoria Grove, born March 21, 1918.
c. Mildred Patricia Grove, born May 6, 1920. Married in 1943 to Harry L. Brewbaker, born January 11, 1919. Two children:
    (1) John Paul Brewbaker, born October 4, 1946
    (2) Patricia Irene Brewbaker, born August 25, 1950. Married July 4, 1969 to David Lee Weaver. Two children:
        (a) Michael A. Weaver: November 10, 1969
        (b) Sara P. Weaver: January 19, 1979
d. Charles Richard Grove, born August 1, 1921. Married in 1942 to Joyce Larue Grimm, born May 4, 1924.

4. Mark Daniel Grove, born March 13, 1894, died November 17, 1976. Married September 19, 1921 to Naomi Wilson, born December 14, 1900, daughter of Edwin Clark Wilson of Sharpsburg, and Pearl Naomi Wyand. Lived in the Boonsboro/Hagerstown area; two children:
    a. Sarah Blessing Grove, born August 23, 1923. Married William James Dwyer, born June 19, 1919, died September 26, 1978. Six children:
        (1) Lois Margaret Dwyer, born May 29, 1946 and married to James Blumenthal, born July 26, 1946. Two children:
            (a) Janice Margaret Blumenthal, born May 11, 1979
            (b) David Arthur Blumenthal, born December 21, 1982
        (2) William James Dwyer, Jr., born February 6, 1948. Married Deborah Quaranto and divorced after one child:

(a) Sarah Margaret Dwyer, born September 8, 1981

(3) Michael Paul Dwyer, born May 2, 1950

(4) Timothy Joseph Dwyer, born January 13, 1952. Married Hilda Moyer, born February 8, 1966. Two children:

(a) Bradley Scott Dwyer: September 2, 1981

(b) Joseph William Dwyer, born September 28, 1985

(5) Daniel Patrick Dwyer, born September 16, 1955. Married Cynthia Lung, born October 18, 1954. One child:

(a) Amy Helen Dwyer, born May 15, 1984

(6) Matthew Dwyer, infant death July 26, 1965

b. Paul Wilson Grove, born November 28, 1924. Married first Mary Patricia Payette, born November 1, 1924 and had six children. Married second Laura DeLauney. His children were:

(1) Marcia Ann Grove, born October 23, 1945. Married Gary Joseph Stallings, born August 2, 1942. Two children:

(a) Peter James Stallings: June 20, 1966

(b) Christopher Gary Stallings, born August 16, 1969

(2) Mary Virginia Grove, born May 10, 1948 and married Dr. Paul Messier, born November 16, 1937. Lived at Falling Waters, West Virginia, and had one child:

(a) Rachael Mary Messier, born September 22, 1982

(3) Mark Stephen Grove, born August 23, 1949. Married Sandra Wolfensburger, born October 13, 1949. Two children:

(a) Jennifer Lynne Grove: October 14, 1975

(b) Mark Daniel Grove: August 30, 1982

(4) Naomi Theresa Grove, born June 6, 1952

(5) Amy Elizabeth Grove, born May 13, 1958 and married to Nelson Bowers, born February 3, 1958. Two children:

(a) Emily Patricia Bowers: August 26, 1981

(b) Daniel Charles Bowers: May 17, 1983

(6) Paula Suzanne Grove, born August 19, 1961

5. James Richard Grove, born September 4, 1896. Married first June 2, 1929 to Helen Laura Waters and had two children. Married second Rosella Miller Fraley. His two children were:
   a. Charles Clarence Grove.
   b. James Richard Grove, Jr., born October 1, 1932.
6. Irving Hugh Grove, born April 19, 1899, died May 10, 1899.
7. Ruth Harriet Grove, born April 11, 1901, died April 5, 1903.

CHILD 6

Ruth Ann Cecilia Biser
1864-1934

This daughter of Daniel A. Biser (1828) and Rose Anna Stottlemyer (1827) was born May 17, 1864, and died April 21, 1934. Married March 1, 1887 to Manassas Lafayette Young of Hagerstown, Maryland, born October 11, 1865, died June 26, 1946. Moved to Upton, Pennsylvania where he worked as a carpenter and contractor. He was injured in an accident, and the family moved to State Line, Pennsylvania, where they farmed, and raised their four children:

1. John Irving Young, born December 20, 1897, died October 12, 1964. Married September 5, 1918 to Edna Mary Kalbflesh, born July 21, 1893, died January 14, 1981, daughter of Frederick Kalbflesh and Mary Shipp.

John and Edna are buried at Rest Haven Cemetery, Hagerstown, Maryland. They had two children:

a. Vivian Rose Young, born November 12, 1919 and married December 25, 1937 to Edward Beksvoort, born March 18, 1913 in Harrlem, Holland and immigrated to America in the 1920s with his parents. One child, who may have been born in New York:
   (1) Judith Young Beksvoort, born April 9, 1939. Married October 25, 1958 to James Vincent Watterson, born August 21, 1937. They had three children:
      (a) Theresa Ann Watterson: March 1, 1960
      (b) Stephen Watterson: October 10, 1962
      (c) Susan Ann Watterson: July 26, 1965
b. Patricia Ann Young, born June 16, 1930. Married July 9, 1949 to Jerome C. Moser, born May 28, 1930. Lived in Hagerstown, and had three children:
   (1) John Wayne Moser, born June 12, 1952. Married November 12, 1977 to Judy Ann McCoy, born November 13, 1958.
   (2) Gary Jerome Moser, born November 8, 1954. Married September 28, 1974 Cynthia Arlene Zartman, born February 12, 1953. One child:
      (a) Todd Jerome Moser: January 10, 1983
   (3) Linda Ann Moser, born September 14, 1956. Married to Morris James Stevenson, Jr., born November 16, 1955; one stepstep and one daughter:
      (a) Michael Paul Stevenson: April 27, 1977
      (b) Ashley Ann Stevenson: May 10, 1984

2. Emil Luther Young, born May 18, 1892, died November 19, 1958. Married to Ruth and lived in Winchester, Virginia. One child:
   a. Elaine Young.

3. Virgil Biser Young, born January 9, 1888, died July 15, 1953. Married; no family information. Buried at Rest Haven Cemetery, Hagerstown.
4. Sarah Ethel Rose Young, born August 19, 1894, died November 8, 1944. Married Aaron Hykes of State Line, Pennsylvania. Living on a farm in that area, she was a school teacher, and they had one son:
   a. Virgil L. Hykes, who lived at Hagerstown.

CHILD 9

Victor Recher Santee Biser
1871-1952

This son of Daniel A. Biser (1828) and Rose Anna Stottlemyer (1827) was born August 9, 1871 on the family farm in Catoctin District, near Wolfsville, in Frederick County, Maryland, as were his siblings, and died January 10, 1952. He began teaching school at the age of nineteen, and was first married January 12, 1893 to Alva Irene Geesey, born 1873, died February 14, 1901, daughter of John Thomas Geesey and Amelia M. Stull. They moved to New York where the last of their five children were born, and his wife died. He was married second to Mary Ann Spangler, born May 5, 1872, died March 22, 1953, daughter of Adam Spangler and Jane Gipe. They had nine children, including three sets of twins. He and his second wife are buried in a cemetery at Strinestown, Pennsylvania; his first wife is buried in the cemetery at old Utica Mills, Frederick County. His children were:

1. Paul Victor Biser, born July 1893, died September 6, 1893.
2. Amelia Marie Biser, born November 12, 1894, died April 14, 1985. Married March 1, 1915 to Bruce Jacobs, born December 13, 1892, died November 20, 1967. One child, adopted:

a. William E. Jacobs, born December 25, 1929. He was married April 7, 1949 to Ruthetta Reachard, born August 8, 1931, and had two children:
  (1) Steven Bradley Jacobs, born April 26, 1952. Married December 16, 1978 to Deborah Lopez, born June 5, 1954. Two children:
    (a) Gregory Stevens Jacobs, born November 19, 1979
    (b) Kristinia Lee Jacobs: March 17, 1982
  (2) Cheryl Marie Jacobs, born December 18, 1957 and married April 19, 1975 to Steven Michael Gross, born August 1, 1956. Two children:
    (a) Melissa Ellen Gross: May 26, 1977
    (b) Lauren Elizabeth Gross, born November 17, 1982.

3. Bruce Recher Biser, born December 5, 1895. Married first Ruth Kraft from Salina, Kansas, and had one son. Married second March 23, 1936 to Doris Merrifield, born June 1, 1903, died March 14, 1986; no children. His son was:
  a. Norman Biser, who was married and had children:
    (1) Paul Biser.
    (2) Andrew Biser, married Vickie and had a son:
      (a) Michael Eric Biser, born 1975

4. Belva Rose Biser, born April 7, 1898, died November 6, 1984. Married Marion Isaac Green, born August 16, 1895, died April 24, 1985, son of Charles Green and Laura Zimmerman. Belva was a teacher in Middletown, Frederick County, and had three children. Buried at Mt. Olivet Cemetery in Frederick. The children were:
  a. Paul James Green, born September 21, 1921. Married March 27, 1947 to Helen R. Zimmerman, born May 6, 1922, daughter of Ephriam Zimmerman and Media Winebrenner. Paul was owner of Farmer's Supply store in Walkersville, and had three children:

(1) Paula Lucretia Green, born Setember 16, 1948 and married to Charles Richard Zimmerman; divorced. Married second to Dennis Jackson. She had two children by her first marriage and a stepson from the second:
   (a) Crista Zimmerman: March 23, 1971
   (b) Charla Marie Zimmerman, born August 10, 1974
   (c) Richard Jackson.
(2) Donald Ephriam Green, born December 24, 1949. Married July 17, 1971 to Marilyn Sue Schaffer, born April 14, 1952, the daughter of Lynn Morris Schaffer and Helen Mae Ayersman. Two daughters:
   (a) Amy Elizabeth Green, born December 27, 1947
   (b) Abby Lynn Green: December 6, 1978
(3) Paul James Green, Jr., born May 6, 1957 and married to Karen Wisner.

b. Charles Victor Green, born April 23, 1923. Married October 3, 1945 to Willie Julia Notnagle, born May 20, 1925, daughter of William Jacob Notnagle and Julia Kemp. Two children:
(1) Charles Victor Green, Jr., born May 13, 1947. Married Sandra Burdette and divorced.
(2) Samuel Isaac Green, born May 8, 1949

c. Margaret Biser Green, born November 1, 1927 and married December 18, 1947 Joseph Louis Lebherz, born April 11, 1927. Four children:
(1) Marian Louise Lebherz, born December 23, 1950. Married Andrew Hawkins and divorced.
(2) Margaret Lenora Lebherz, born March 15, 1952. Married July 18, 1980 Roger Herrmann, born December 10, 1947, who had two children from an earlier marriage:

(a) Chez Herrmann, born April 3, 1972
(b) Flint Herrmann, born March 15, 1978

(3) Joseph Louis Lebherz, Jr., born February 12, 1954. Married August 2, 1980 Angela Marie Coffman, born September 27, 1955, and had one child:

(a) Laura Jane Lebherz, born July 23, 1984

(4) Daniel Walsh Lebherz, born August 4, 1955. Married May 2, 1981 to Elaine Marie Kochanowski, born December 10, 1954, and had two children:

(a) Jennifer Marie Lebherz: August 1, 1982
(b) Daniel Walsh Lebherz, Jr., born January 17, 1984

5. Silas E. Biser, born January 20, 1901, died August 19, 1950, single.
6. Theodore McCauley Biser, born December 8, 1904, died May 26, 1986. Married first to Ethel Hein and had six children. Married second to Irene Lawrence, born February 25, 1917, and had two more children. Irene had two children at the time of their marriage, who are listed as the last two children in the family:

a. Betty Biser, born July 25, 1934. Married first Harry L. Shoop and had two children. Married second to Charles Blauser. Her children were:

(1) Burton L. Shoop, born November 18, 1956 and married to Deborah Wheeler.
(2) Brad E. Shoop, born December 12, 1959

b. Carolyn Biser, born August 4, 1935. Married first to Lee Matherly, and had two children. Married second to Leroy Emenheiser, and had one child:

(1) Debbie Matherly.
(2) Cathy Matherly.
(3) Chantay Emenheiser.

c. Timothy Biser, born May 16, 1937. Married first to Janice Sammon and had two children, divorced. He was married second to Debra Starner who had four children. His children were:
   (1) Teddy Biser.
   (2) Joan Biser.
d. Maxine Biser, born May 11, 1939. Married first to William Sheffer and had a son. Married second Charles Gurreri and had a son. Married third Charles Flaharty. Her children were:
   (1) Michael Sheffer.
   (2) Charles Gurreri.
e. Lila Mae Biser, born May 7, 1941. Married Charles Michaels and had a son:
   (1) Ricardo Michaels.
f. Eugene Clifford Biser, born February 25, 1945 and died 1965 from accidental gunshot wound; single.
g. Victor Robert Biser, born November 27, 1948 and married to Bonnie; one child. He was married twice more: to Ginger by whom he had a child; and third to Joy. His children were:
   (1) Shonta Biser, born 1968
   (2) Shane Biser, born 1977
h. Renee Mae Biser, born April 5, 1950. Married Zane Busser and had a child:
   (1) Tammy Lynn Busser, born April 26, 1977
i. Nancy Jean Lawrence, born May 19, 1935. Married Jimmie Hartnett and had four children:
   (1) Patricia Hartnett.
   (2) Nancy Hartnett.
   (3) Kathleen Hartnett.
   (4) Colleen Hartnett.
j. Andrea Kayrene Lawrence, born October 13, 1944.

7. Margaret Biser, born March 3, 1906. Married to Norman Latimer Crone, born June 4, 1906, and died February 7, 1975. They lived near York, Pennsylvania; two children:
    a. Norman Latimer Crone, Jr., born July 20, 1930 and married first to Jeanette; two children. Married second to Charlene Myers and had three children:
        (1) Pamela Crone, born 1953
        (2) Joseph Crone, born 1955
        (3) Susan Crone, born June 6, 1957
        (4) Sandra Crone, born March 3, 1959
        (5) Norman Latimer Crone, III, born February 1, 1961.
    b. Robert Eugene Crone, born September 5, 1937 and lived one day.
8. Charlotte Biser, an infant death.
9. Mary Magdeline Biser, twin, born December 15, 1909. Married to Clarence Holder and had a son:
    a. James Lee Holder, born September 12, 1930, and married to Beverly Brink. Two children:
        (1) James Lee Holder, Jr., born July 14, 1960 and married to Kelly. Two children:
            (a) Ericka Holder, born July 16, 1979
            (b) Erin Holder, born January 17, 1982
        (2) Terry Holder, born March 21, 1957
10. Robert Biser, twin, born December 15, 1909, and died 1931 while in the service; single.
11. Charlotte Biser, twin, infant death.
12. Catherine Biser, twin, infant death.
13. Grace Biser, twin, born February 27, 1912; infant death
14. Blanche Biser, twin, born February 27, 1912. Married to John Sterner and had four children:
    a. Patsy Sterner, born December 20, 1935
    b. Donald E. Sterner, infant death March 31, 1938

c. Mary Jane Sterner, born October 31, 1939. Married Mervin Haring, born January 31, 1941. They had three children:
   (1) Scott Haring, born June 28, 1963
   (2) Karla Haring, born December 25, 1967
   (3) Shawn Haring, born April 12, 1970

d. Terry Lee Sterner.

CHAPTER 6

Stottlemyer Families of Frederick County

Elizabeth Stottlemyer
died c.1871

Elizabeth apparently survived her husband, who is not known to us at this time. Her will is dated July 17, 1871 and entered for record August 1, 1871 in Book SGC-1 at folio 176 in Frederick County, Maryland. She leaves to the one son named following, the house and lot, plus two cows and hogs. The residue is to go to "my children now living," to be equally divided between them, but fails to provide any names. There were apparently several children, one of whom was:

1. James Lewis Stottlemyer, who received the house and lot, two cows and two hogs. The residue was to be divided between all the children who survived their mother.

Joseph Stottlemyer
died 1864

Joseph's will was dated March 26, 1864, probated April 4, 1864, and recorded in will book TLMc1 at folio 26 in the Frederick County records. He does not mention a wife, but does name three sons and a daughter. He also provides that the residue of his estate, after the specific bequests, is to be sold and distributed and appoints Joseph Stottlemyer of D. to manage that task. The residue consists of the home farm, a wood lot purchased from John Stottlemyer, and a town lot at Cavetown, in Washington County. The children were:

1. Amanda Elizabeth Stottlemyer, married June 24, 1863 to William Himes. She received the lands called *Low Spring* and *Bakers Lot*, containing 21 acres. Also a wood lot of

about 15 acres, to be surveyed out of the Hays farm. It appears from cemetery records that Amanda Elizabeth was the second wife of William Himes. At the Wolfsville United Brethren Church, there are burials that appear to be this family. William Himes was born c.1826 and died July 16, 1898. There is also Elizabeth A., born 1822, died June 18, 1861 at the age of 39 years and 8 days, indicated as his wife. Also, Amanda E. is buried there as his wife, born 1845, died July 16, 1906. There are three sons buried with the family group:

a. William T. H. Himes, born 1875, died October 19, 1897.
b. David E. Himes, born 1883, died September 16, 1957 (listed as buried at Ellerton Brethren)
c. George R. Himes, born 1886, died October 25, 1890

2. Washington Hamilton Stottlemyer, the eldest son, received *The Forest Lot* and lands purchased from Wilson Hays, less that portion described above.
3. Joseph Stottlemyer received the "land left to me by my father, known as *Preaching.*"
4. Denton Stottlemyer was to receive his bequest at the time he reached the age of 25 years. Hence, he was born after 1839.

John E. Stottlemyer
1865-

John E. was born c.1865 and is buried at the cemetery of the Foxville Lutheran Church in Frederick County. His wife was Effie M., born c.1866, and there are two daughters buried with their parents. There were perhaps other children:

1. Mary E. Stottlemyer, died August 5, 1898 at the age of two months and five days.
2. Margaret R. Stottlemyer, born 1905, died October 28, 1907 at the age of two years, four months.

Joseph Stottlemyer
1824-1889

This Joseph was born c.1824 and died February 28, 1889 in Frederick County, Maryland. He is buried with his wife at the Ellerton Brethren Church. Married in 1857 to Amanda Grossnickle, born March 6, 1837, died March 24, 1912. She was a daughter of John Grossnickle, Sr. (1783) and Mary Hauver. One son is buried with them; there were perhaps other children:

1. John Stottlemyer, died March 30, 1871, aged three days

Joshua Stottlemyer
1823-1887

Joshua was born c.1823 and died June 24, 1887, aged 64 years, 2 months and 12 days; buried at the Ellerton Brethren Church with his wife. She was Malinda, born c.1837 and died August 10, 1890, aged 53 years, 4 months and 16 days. Two sons are buried with them; there may be other children:

1. Joshua Newton Stottlemyer, born c.1873, died December 25, 1880, aged 7 years, 3 months and 29 days.
2. John J. C. Stottlemyer, born c.1876, died January 26, 1881, aged 5 years, and 14 days.

Mary Stottlemyer
1770-

Reference to Mary is found in records of the Mormon Church. She is said there to have been married to Christian Harman, born May 18, 1770 in Frederick County, Maryland, son of Marcus Harman and Christina Leatherman Getz. He married second Anna Maria Morningstar, born November 23, 1774 in Frederick County. He had children, perhaps born in Washington County, Maryland:

1. John George Harman, born c.1792
2. Jacob Harman, born c.1800. Married April 1, 1824 in the county to Margaret Rebecca Goodman.
3. William Harman, born c.1805

Benjamin E. Stottlemyer
1863-1931

This Benjamin was born c.1863 and died 1931; buried at the Oak Hill Church of God, north of Woodsville, Frederick County, Maryland. His wife Ida E. is buried with him; she was born c.1866 and died November 17, 1910, age 44 years, 9 months and 18 days. One daughter is there also:

1. Lillian V. Stottlemyer, born 1905, died 1923

C. Columbus Stottlemyer
1857-1931

Buried at Wolfsville United Brethren Church, Frederick County, Maryland, C. Columbus was born October 5, 1857 and died February 13, 1931. His wife Sarah P. C. is buried with him; she was born July 12, 1865 and died November 15, 1952. One son is buried there also:

1. C. Clyde Stottlemyer, born September 25, 1886

Walter L. Stottlemyer
1871-1940

Walter was born c.1871, died 1940; buried at Wolfsville Lutheran Church. His wife is buried there also; she was Annie C., born 1871, died 1940. There are three daughters buried with them, and there may have been other children:

1. Alma Grace Stottlemyer, born c.1896, died October 30, 1918 at the age of 22 years, 16 days.

2. Margaret E. Stottlemyer, born 1909, died September 23, 1909 at the age of 3 months and 19 days.
3. Helen L. Stottlemyer, born c.1911, died November 22, 1918 at the age of 7 years, 6 months and 14 days.

William T. H. Stottlemyer
1862-1898

William T. H. was born c.1862 and died January 3, 1898 at the age of 36 years, 3 months and 17 days. Buried at the Wolfsville United Brethren Church. His wife is buried with him; she was Mary Ellen, born c.1859, died June 13, 1955 at the age of 96 years, 3 months and 25 days. One son and a daughter are buried with them:

1. Josiah Lester Stottlemyer, born November 26, 1886, died August 20, 1887
2. Virgie E. Stottlemyer, born 1891, died September 9, 1891 at the age of 4 months and 14 days

Sarah A. Stottlemyer
1840-1900

Her parents are as yet unknown, but cemetery records indicate that Sarah was born c.1840 and died August 15, 1900. She was married to Hezekiah C. Putman, probably in Frederick County, Maryland. He was born March 4, 1835 and died March 2, 1908; both are buried at Mt. Oliver cemetery in Frederick. They had at least one daughter:

1. Minnie M. Putman, born 1878, died 1942; buried at Mt. Olivet cemetery in Frederick with her husband and one young daughter. Married to Charles H. Klipp, born January 29, 1869, died 1939, son of Henry Klipp (1846), and Sarah Miss (daughter of Lewis Miss and Elizabeth Lutz). Charles H. Klipp was engaged in farming, and in putting up monuments. He later built three dwellings in West

Fifth Street of Frederick City, and lived in one of them until he moved back to a farm near the city. He was also a contractor, building roads and railroads. Among his many projects was the paved road at Braddock Heights. Minnie and Charles had five children:

a. Sarah E. Klipp, born May 31, 1903, died March 2, 1908 and buried with her parents.
b. Nellie M. Klipp.
c. Goldie R. Klipp.
d. Lillie H. Klipp.
e. Margaret L. Klipp.

Catherine Stottlemyer
1791-

Catherine is shown in Mormon records as having been married to Daniel P. Barackman, born January 1, 1790 in Frederick County, Maryland, died April 30, 1864 in Livingston County, Illinois. He was the son of Christoph Bergman (sic) and Anna Maria Bantz, and was apparently married second April 28, 1816 to Mary Pettinger. At least one son, born Frederick:

1. Bartley Barackman.

Mahala Stottlemyer
1834-1879

Mahala is reported in records of western Maryland as having been born c.1834 and died in Frederick County, May 29, 1879. She was married April 11, 1863 in Frederick County, Maryland, to Moses Lee Hurley, born c.1835, son of John Hurley (1793). He was the father of at least one son, and probably other children:

1. L. Wilson Hurley, born c.1858 in Maryland and married to Genora Louisa Toms Draper

Ira V. Stottlemyer
1872-1953

Ira was born August 30, 1872, died April 27, 1953, and was buried at the Wolfsville United Brethren Church. He was married to Mary Viola Martin, born November 26, 1873. They had children:

1. Eva I. Stottlemyer, born December 12, 1895, died December 26, 1995 at Fahreny Keedy Memorial Home in Boonesboro. Married September 8, 1934 to Leslie Irving Morgan, born November 23, 1885, died March 24, 1973, son of Irving Recher Morgan (1860) and Ida Mary Ellen Smith (1866). Lester Irving Morgan was also married to Carrie Fox.
2. Mary L. Stottlemyer, born c.1911, died January 20, 1996 at the age of 85, at her home in Hagerstown. Married to Irvin Paul Gish, Sr., who died in 1964. Children:
   a. Mary F. Gish, married Snook.
   b. Irvin Paul Gish, Jr.
3. Martha E. Stottlemyer, married to Rice of Mount Lena.
4. Frank V. Stottlemyer, of Wolfsville.
5. Glenna Stottlemyer, married Slenker.
6. Ira Stottlemyer.
7. Elvin Stottlemyer.

Sarah Ann Stottlemyer
1842-

We have not determined her parentage, but Sarah Ann was married April 16, 1860 in Frederick County to Benjamin Shuff, Jr. (1837) and had at least one daughter:

1. Lucretia Shuff, born 1862, and died 1941. Married three times: first to John William Hooper (1862) and second to David Barkman, Jr. (1830). She was married third to Henry Levi Brandenburg, born December 13, 1853 on

the family farm in Catoctin District of Frederick County, Maryland, and died April 12, 1928, the son of Samuel Brandenburg (1824) and Julia Ann Catharine Grossnickle (1829). Henry Levi is buried at the Ellerton Brethren Church, with his wife; and his parents. He worked on the family farm prior to purchasing a ninety-three acre farm about a half mile north of Wolfsville. He operated a large sawmill on his property, providing lumber for many of the buildings in the valley. He was first married to Louisa C. Grossnickle, born July 5, 1856, died May 16, 1914, daughter of George P. Grossnickle (1830) and Sarah Ann Grossnickle (1834). Levi, listed only by that name, appears as head of the household in the 1880 census of Frederick County, Maryland, born c.1855. His wife was Louisa, born c.1857, and they then had three children. There is a will of one L. H. Brandenburg, dated February 17, 1926 and probated April 25, 1928; filed in liber GES2 at folio 351 in Frederick; believed to be that of Henry Levi. Although it has only initials in the will, it is indexed under the given name Levi. In the will of Henry Levi the wife is named Lucretia, and Lloyd R. Brandenburg is named as Executor. The 1900 census for Frederick County lists the family again, although the Soundex film at the Archives was faint and difficult to read. He appeared to be listed as Harry L. Brandenburg, with his first wife, Louisa C., and ten children. The couple appear in the 1920 census for Frederick County, with just one son, Harry. Henry Levi and Louisa had as many as sixteen children, all but one reaching maturity. Lucretia had at least one daughter from her first marriage:

a. Minnie A. Hooper, married to Alvey P. Harshman, born February 22, 1878 near Wolfsville, the son of John T. Harshman (1841) and Nancy J. Bowman (1846). One son:
   (1) John W. Harshman.

William Hamilton Stottlemyer
1837-1905

William Hamilton was born c.1837 in Frederick County, and died May 7, 1905 at the age of 68 years, 9 months and 15 days, and is buried at the Ellerton Brethren Church. His wife is also buried there; she was Susannah, born c.1836 and died July 16, 1913 at the age of 77 years, 1 month and 29 days. They had children:

1. Clarence B. Stottlemyer, born 1856, of whom more.
2. William H. Stottlemyer, born c.1866, died April 25, 1912 at the age of 46 years, 8 months and 1 day.
3. Levi Stottlemyer, born 1871, died May 1, 1871 at the age of one month.

Clarence B. Stottlemyer
1856-1906

Clarence was a son of William Hamilton Stottlemyer (1837), who was an early settler in the Catoctin District of Frederick County, Maryland. Clarence was born on his father's farm April 1, 1856, and died July 10, 1906. He is buried in the Ellerton Brethren Church cemetery on Meeting House Road. He remained on his father's farm until after his marriage. He was married to Lydia A. Cordelia Warrenfeltz, born November 29, 1859, died May 6, 1935, daughter of Ezra A. Warrenfeltz (1815) and Lydia Ann Biser (1822). After marriage, Clarence worked for others until he accumulated enough to purchase a 112 acre farm from Lawrence Easterday, on which he lived until his death. His will was dated April 26, 1906 and probated July 23, 1906, recorded in will book WBC1 at folio 273 in Frederick. It is very simple, leaving his entire estate to his wife. Six children, and perhaps seven according to the history of the Biser family:

1. Welty M. Stottlemyer, born 1880, died 1945; buried at Ellerton Brethren Church. He was a farmer in Catoctin District, married to Bertha M., born 1877, died 1949 and buried with her husband.
2. Levi E. Stottlemyer, also a farmer in Catoctin. Probably same as Levi E., born November 12, 1883, buried at the Ellerton Brethren Church.
3. Ida L. Stottlemyer.
4. Alice V. Stottlemyer, married to David W. Stollemyer, who was not related.
5. David W. Stottlemyer, perhaps. Named in a history of the Biser family, but believed not to be correct; perhaps confused with the husband of Alice V., just above.
6. Lester A. Stottlemyer.
7. Clarence B. Stottlemyer, Jr.

John Stottlemyer
1818-1878

John was born February 7, 1818 in Frederick County, Maryland, and died November 30, 1878. He is buried with his wife at the Wolfsville United Brethren Church. Married March 7, 1844 to Susanna Elizabeth Bussard, born May 30, 1822 and died October 22, 1892, daughter of John Householder Bussard and Elizabeth DeLaughter. The will of this John Stottlemyer was dated November 25, 1878, and entered for record in Book JRR-1 at folio 327 in Frederick County, Maryland. It names only his wife, Susan, and refers to some property located in Cavetown, Washington County, Maryland. Several children, however, born in Frederick County:

1. Mary A. Stottlemyer, born c.1845; died January 15, 1902. Married to Josiah Harp, born February 25, 1834, died June 1, 1894; buried at Ellerton Brethren Church, son of George Harp, Jr. and Catherine Poffenberger. He had first been married to Mary Ann Rebecca Kesselring,

born 1833, died August 17, 1869; buried there also. Josiah and Mary had children, all born in Maryland:

a. Emma Harp, born 1872, died August 9, 1873
b. Ettie Harp, born December 20, 1876, died August 20, 1877
c. Eva Mae Harp, born March 17, 1879, died May 26, 1969. Married March 22, 1900 to George Emerson Mowen, born April 19, 1878 in Maryland.
d. Albert Harp, born about 1881.
e. Edith Harp, born January 27, 1882. Married Elmer Granville Brandenburg, born October 26, 1880, died May 20, 1957. A merchant in Hagerstown, he was the son of Marion Granville Brandenburg (1857) and Laura Catherine Routzahn (1858). They were found in the 1920 census for Hagerstown, Washington County, Maryland. Children:
    (1) Albert Harp Brandenburg, born June 5, 1905. Married March 28, 1928 to Carnella Brewer, born June 5, 1905.
    (2) Helen Adele Brandenburg: 1908, died 1977
    (3) Vivian May Brandenburg: March 12, 1912
f. Walter C. Harp, born 1885, died October 30, 1889
g. Esther Harp, born June 11, 1885, died June 12, 1889.

2. Howard R. Stottlemyer, born c.1846.
3. Cornelia Stottlemyer, born November 24, 1847, and died August 5, 1929. Married to Daniel Marcellus Duvall, born June 21, 1836, died June 28, 1925. Children:
    a. Edwin Clyde Duvall, born April 9, 1882, and died January 6, 1956
    b. Carrie Villa Duvall, born April 26, 1884, died October 19, 1970. Married Jesse Karl Sherwood, born December 25, 1881 in Maryland, and had at least two children:
        (1) Helen Virginia Sherwood: February 25, 1913.

(2) Son Sherwood, married Helen Elizabeth Mallow, born October 11, 1919.

4. Savilla Catherine Stottlemyer, born July 1, 1852 and died March 11, 1950. Married November 10, 1874 to Henry Samuel Myers, born September 3, 1850 in Maryland, and died there January 23, 1920. Children, born Maryland:
   a. Anna Belle Myers, born April 4, 1881, died January 8, 1963. Married to Albert Reuben Sherwood, born January 8, 1879 in Maryland. They had four children, one of whom was:
      (1) Albert Maurice Sherwood, born c.1924
   b. Charles Myers, born about 1883
   b. Frank Myers, born about 1885.
   c. Mack Myers, born November 4, 1890, died December 5, 1974. Married June 25, 1921 to Gladys I. Whitlock, born August 28, 1891 in Maryland.
5. Annie Stottlemyer, born about 1854
6. John Rufus Stottlemyer, born February 9, 1859, and died December 10, 1930 Frederick County, Maryland. Married at Middletown April 9, 1884 to Malinda Ellen Poffenberger, born June 2, 1859, and died April 22, 1930. Buried at Wolfsville United Brethren Church. They had children, born Frederick County:
   a. Emory Fleet Stottlemyer, born April 4, 1885, died October 4, 1971. Married June 17, 1908 to Mary Rae Kelbaugh, born July 7, 1887, and had at least six children, including:
      (1) Rachel Stottlemyer, born April 29, 1909 near Thurmont, Maryland, died February 24, 1997 at Homewood Retirement Center, Williamsport, Maryland. A graduate of Strayer Business College in Baltimore, she studied voice at Peabody Conservatory and at Hood College in Frederick. She was active in a number of societies associated with music, including service

as a director of the Baltimore Civic Opera Association. For twenty-six years, she served as a director of the Hagerstown Salvation Army, and received the Beulah Meyers Award for twenty-five years of voluntary service. Married to Dr. William M. Brish, former Superintendent of Washington County Public Schools. Three daughters:

(a) Marianne Brish, married Evett.

(b) Margaret Brish, married Wagner.

(c) Marcia Brish, married Shenk.

(2) James Lee Stottlemyer, born December 23, 1919 in Maryland, died December 10, 1970

(3) John Stottlemyer.

(4) Paul Stottlemyer.

b. Vada Anna Stottlemyer, born August 7, 1886. Married February 19, 1905 to Grover C. Hurley, born April 14, 1885 in Maryland, and had at least three children, two of whom were:

(1) Eva Marie Hurley, born December 23, 1906

(2) Ralph Emory Hurley, born February 12, 1913

7. George Reuben Stottlemyer, born January 27, 1862, died March 12, 1930 in Frederick County. Buried Wolfsville United Brethren Church with his wife. Married December 29, 1891 to Lillie Rose Young, born April 22, 1868, died May 7, 1942, daughter of Ezra Young. The will of George Reuben, dated January 10, 1929 was probated March 24, 1930 and recorded in will book CHB 1 at folio 211 in Frederick County. It names his wife, and four of the children; two died quite young:

a. Gail Price Stottlemyer, born August 17, 1892. Married November 15, 1932 to Frances Weber. Named in his father's will.

b. Key Y. Stottlemyer, born 1894, died November 2, 1895

c. Belva Ruth Stottlemyer, born February 7, 1896. Married September 3, 1927 William Walter Troxler, born June 19, 1887. Named in her father's will.
d. Rudolph M. Stottlemyer, born 1898, died August 6, 1898
e. G. Reginald Stottlemyer, named in the will.
f. Donald E. Stottlemyer, born October 23, 1904.

8. Emma E. Stottlemyer, born April 5, 1867, died September 30, 1950 in Frederick County. Married John Elias Moser, born April 13, 1864. At least one son:
   a. Hubert Moser, born c.1888, died February 12, 1967 in Maryland. Married to Della L. Coss, and had at least one child.

John Stottlemyer
1820-1874

This John Stottlemyer, of the many to bear the name, was found with his descendants in ancestral records of the Mormon Church, at the Family History Center in Kensington, Montgomery County, Maryland. It is there reported that he was born c.1820 in Maryland (or perhaps Virginia), and died December 22, 1874 in Myers Township, Grundy County, Missouri. He was married November 21, 1846 to Priscilla Hexinberger, born May 18, 1828 in Pennsylvania, and died April 17, 1918 in Joplin, Missouri, daughter of John Hexinberger. Her birth in Pennsylvania suggests that John may have been born in the western counties of Maryland, near the Pennsylvania border. They apparently moved soon after marriage into neighboring areas of West Virginia and Virginia, and finally to Illinois. They had children, including:

1. Caroline Stottlemyer, born c.1847 in West Virginia and died July 20, 1854
2. John Edgar Stottlemyer, born October 8, 1850 in West Virginia. Married three times: July 28, 1871 to Martha

A. Carr; November 7, 1886 to Elizabeth Varnell; and May 29, 1904 to Amy Stallcup.

3. Mary Ann Stottlemyer, born January 17, 1852 in Virginia, and died July 10, 1871. Married August 11, 1870 to George W. Johnson.
4. Susanna Stottlemyer, born January 3, 1854 in Virginia, died April 15, 1917. Married March 14, 1872 to James Mansfield Batson.
5. David Stottlemyer, born June 30, 1856 in Virginia, died 1937. Married twice: January 1, 1882 to Amaiah Batson and second December 18, 1890 to Laura B. Holden.
6. Rachel Stottlemyer, born February 10, 1858 in Virginia, died 1910. Married three times: October 22, 1870 to James W. Batson (or John W.), second to Joe Payne, and third to Chambers.
7. William Stottlemyer, born March 4, 1860 in Virginia and died October 8, 1863
8. Sarah Stottlemyer, born January 6, 1862 in Virginia and died February 26, 1899. Married to Rook.
9. James M. Stottlemyer, born June 10, 1865 in Illinois, and died 1911. Married twice: first October 20, 1891 to Margaret Ann Volmer, and second June 8, 1909 Myrtle Ragains.
10. General Jackson Stottlemyer, born July 14, 1867 in Illinois, died January 20, 1953 in Green Township, Utica County, Missouri. Married in Livingston County, Missouri March 25, 1888 to Almina Batson, born April 14, 1866 in Mercer County, Missouri. They had children, born in Missouri:
    a. John Leonard Stottlemyer, born October 23, 1890, and reportedly married four times: Stella Mae, Anna, Millie Scholl, and Opal.
    b. Hannah Rebecca Stottlemyer, born 1892. Married twice: Roy Williams and Mike Naughton.

c. Robert Emmitt Stottlemyer, born October 4, 1896. Married Mabel Alberta Schneider.
d. Son Stottlemyer, married Helen Martha Puschert, born July 11, 1902 at Britzy, Germany. At least four children.
e. Samuel Jackson Stottlemyer, born May 13, 1902.
f. Homer Orval Stottlemyer, born May 6, 1905.
g. Willie Stottlemyer.
h. Ray Stottlemyer.

11. Nancy Lewis Stottlemyer, born March 6, 1873 in Missouri, died 1935. Married twice: to John R. Brooks and second to Warren Coglizer.

Marriage Licenses of Frederick County, Maryland

The following are all those persons having the surname of Stottlemyer (by several variant spellings as well), listed in the Index of Marriages, 1778-1865, for Frederick County. Compiled by an unknown clerk, there are references to the original license book. Those books could not be found in the courthouse at Frederick, nor in the State Hall of Records in Annapolis. The only remaining information appears to be the names of the individuals, and the date the marriage was issued. Names in the left column bear the surname Stottlemyer.

Male	Spouse
Alice V.	Md 01/29/1880 John Smith, a butcher.
Catherine	Md 04/23/1844 Joshua Lane, Jr.
Clara V.	Md 10/05/1871 Daniel Warrenfeltz.
Daniel	Md 07/21/1854Elizabeth Harshman.
Daniel	Md 12/27/1855 Catherine Fultz
David	Md 04/15/1808 Jemima Castle

David	Md 04/06/1814 Mary Curfman
Elizabeth	Md 11/19/1811 Levin Hurley
Elizabeth	Md 06/11/1849 William Himes
Emaline	Md 08/31/1848 George Grissinger
George	Md 11/06/1779 Catherine Calon
George	Md 09/19/1845 Mary A. Mullen
Hamilton	Md 08/31/1855 Susanna Hauver
Hiram	Md 11/01/1837 Elizabeth Ambrose
Hiram L.	Md 03/17/1860 Henrietta Clayton Hager
Jacob	Md 01/25/1785 Hedwick Shoemaker
James	Md 01/21/1834 Mary Boyer
James C.	Md 01/22/1849 Mary J. Harper
John	Md 07/27/1798 Sarah Michael
John	Md 12/19/1819 Susanna Wolf. Found also in Washington County
John, Jr.	Md 05/25/1828 Mary Hay
Joseph	Md 03/31/1848 Hannah Hauver
Joseph	Md 01/21/1814 Mary Baker
Joseph	Md 11/04/1849 Martha Ann Rebecca Harley
Leah	Md 03/08/1836 John Jones
Magdalene	Md 12/23/1809 Philip Baker
Mahaly	Md 04/11/1853 Moses Lee Hurley
Malinda	Md 11/11/1840 James K. Wolf
Margaret	Md 10/31/1842 Henry Ridenour
Martha	Md 06/03/1865 James K. P. Wolf
Martin	Md Alice Murphy, d/o Horace L. Murphy (1824) and Charlotte D. Thompson.
Mary	Md 10/05/1831 Jacob Heck
Mary	Md 01/07/1851 Joseph Warner
Mary Ann	Md 01/16/1864 James Oliver Harshman
Nelson Lee	Md 12/28/1852 Sarah Ann Hurley
Polly	Md 10/01/1816 John Wilson
S. Ann	Md 12/22/1853 George Harman
Sarah A.	Md 02/02/1863 Elias Delauder of Henry
Sarah Ann	Born 10/08/1808, md 03/15/1833 John Henry Harshman
Susan	Md 02/10/1845 John Kinney
Susan	Md 02/14/1851 Hezekiah Palmer

Susan M.	Md 12/08/1872 Franklin Brunner.
Susanna	Md 03/02/1805 Francis Richmond
Wilson	Md 03/16/1859 Catharine Shuff
William H.	Md 07/30/1859 Mary C. Palmer

Miscellaneous Records of Frederick County

The following are one-liner type pieces of information found along the way. The individual in the left column bears the Stottlemyer surname, by birth or marriage.

Individual	Information
A. J.	Born 02/14/1863, died 11/11/1929. Buried Mt. Olivet, Frederick, Maryland. Wife Sadie A., born 03/10/1870.
Asa P.	Born 1889, buried at Wolfsville United Baptist Church. Wife Edna B. born 1891, died 1951
Clarence W.	Born 12/24/1900, buried Ellerton Brethren Ch.
D. Franklin	Born 01/19/1892, died 07/21/1959. Buried in the Mt. Olivet cemetery, Frederick. Wife Myrtle M. born 04/09/1894, died 05/24/1950
Dorothy V.	Born 1927, died 03/19/1907, age 0-5-6. Buried at Middletown Lutheran Church.
Edward M.	Born 1870, died 1943, buried Marvin Chapel Methodist Church, Mt. Airy, Md Wife Laura V., born 1869, died 1941.
Ellen S.	Born c.1858, died 01/31/1886, age 28-8-18. Buried Wolfsville Lutheran Ch. W/o Charles.
Elva M.	Born c.1876, died 04/02/1912, age 36-8-23. W/o John M. C. Buried at Mt. Bethel Methodist Ch.
Faith Irene	Born 1956, died 02/04/1956 at 29 days. Buried at Oak Hill Church of God north of Woodsville.
Francis E.	Born June 15, 1920, died July 12, 1921. Buried Wolfsville United Brethren.
Grover M.	Born 09/15/1888, died 03/22/1940. Buried at the Pleasant Walk United Brethren Church.

Harlen P.	Born 1866, died 1931, buried Wolfsville United Baptist Church. Wife Elizabeth C., born 1874, died 1939
Hiram	Born 07/31/1846, died 12/20/1917. Wife Mary Wolf, born 03/06/1851, died 02/27/1937.
Hiram	Born 01/04/1848, died 02/21/1918. Buried at the Pleasant Walk United Brethren Church. His wife Sophia C., born 05/08/1853, died 04/05/1937
Hiram J.	Born 05/03/1844, died 05/06/1902. Mt. Olivet cemetery, Frederick.
Ira W.	Born 07/29/1896, died 12/31/1958. Mt. Olivet cemetery, Frederick.
Irving R.	Born 1872, died 1946; minister, buried Ellerton Brethren Church. Wife Annie S., born 1873, died 1958.
Jennie	Md Henry Carlton Dutrow, born 05/17/1868 at Frederick Co, died 02/27/1944. At least three children.
John	Born 09/26/1791, died 07/17/1867. Buried at the Ellerton Brethren Church.
John H.	Born c.1810, died 04/27/1873. Wolfsville Lutheran Church.
John M.	Born 02/24/1829, died 12/11/1901. Buried at the Legore cemetery. His wife Barbara A., born 11/28/1843, died 04/03/1904.
John R.	Born 10/06/1870, died 07/11/1954. Buried at Mt. Olivet cemetery, Frederick. Wife Susan E., born 05/06/1876, died 07/01/1948.
Joseph	Born c.1843, died 08/31/1909; buried Wolfsville United Brethren. Wife Martha A., born c.1848, died 03/31/1919.
Joseph D.	Born 1851, died 09/02/1852 aged 1 year and 22 days. Buried Jerusalem cemetery near Myersville s/o John W. and Mary B. Stottlemyer.
Joseph D.	Born 1904, died 03/14/1904, aged 4 months and 5 days. Son of E. J. and A. D. Stottlemyer.
Martin L.	Born 11/03/1876, died 06/02/1952, buried at the New Market Methodist Church.

Mary M.	Born c.1852, died 02/21/1856, aged 4-1-23. D/o Thomas and Sarah Stottlemyer. Buried Ellerton.
Newton A.	Born 1904, died 06/27/1904, aged 0-5-27. Son of J. N. and Minnie. Middletown Lutheran Church.
Orville H.	08/08/1887 to 04/01/1947; buried Fort Richie German Church. Two wives: Mettie G., born c.1893, died 05/20/1923, aged 29-10-24; Mazie I., born 07/22/1899.
Stacy M.	Born 09/19/1892, died 10/14/1917. Wolfsville United Brethren.
Thomas J.	Born 08/18/1906, died 09/25/1946. Oak Hill Church of God north of Woodsboro.
Thomas J.	Born 07/29/1937, died 02/06/1939. Oak Hill Church of God north of Woodsboro.

CHAPTER 7

Stottlemyer Families of Washington County

Susan Stottlemyer
1804-1857

We do not know her parents, but Susan Stottlemyer was born June 8, 1804, apparently in Washington County, Maryland, and died June 11, 1857, and is buried at Union cemetery, West End, Bedford County, Pennsylvania. She was married in Washington County March 27, 1821 to Nathan Hurley, born October 29, 1798 in Prince George's County, Maryland, son of William Hurley (1739) and Sarah Soper (1756). After the death of William Hurley, his widow had married secondly in Prince George's, October 3, 1801, to Paul Summers. The family moved to Washington County, Maryland, where Paul Summers died c.1846.

Nathan is mentioned on page 307 of *History of Bedford, Somerset and Fulton Counties, Pennsylvania,* dated 1884. There, it is said that he was born in Maryland in 1798, removed to Bedford County (later Blair County), Pennsylvania in 1837, and thence to Centre County, where he was living as of 1884. It is reported that two of his sons, John and Webster, died in the "late war." William, another of his sons, was then keeping the hotel at New Enterprise, which was built by Samuel Stayer in 1873. William served in Hancock's Corp from September, 1862 to June 15, 1865, and was wounded in service. On page 234 of the book referenced, Nathan was listed as a member of the first Directors of Juniata Township in 1853.

Nathan Hurley also appears in a deed from Martin Dumphrey, dated 1848 and indexed as being found in deed book H at page 471 in the land records of Bedford County, PA. I was unable to find the deed under that index when I visited the courthouse, but later learned that it is actually to be found in book X at page 471, and that there, Nathan is said to be from Warriors Mark, Huntingdon County, Pennsylvania. Nathan later appears in two deeds, both dated March 22, 1865. In one, he conveys 213 acres of land to Henry Horn, recorded in deed book AL at page 308. The second deed is an assignment of lease to Catherine Robb, and filed in deed book AL at page 336. In both of these cases, Nathan Hurley signed with his mark, and his wife Mary Maria Hurley also signed with her mark. We know that Nathan's wife, Susan, or Susanna, Stottlemyer Hurley, died in 1857, so it appears that Nathan has married for a second time.

Nathan appears to have actually been married three times. He is listed in the 1870 census of the borough of Unionville, Centre County, Pennsylvania, at the age of 72, with one Rebecca Gearhart at the age of 55 (born c.1815), listed as housekeeper. In the 1880 census of the same locale, we now find Nathan, with a wife named Rebecca, "keeping house." Obviously, they were married between 1870 and 1880.

While we still do not know the date of death nor where Nathan was buried, it appears likely that he died in Centre County, Pennsylvania; and is probably buried there.

An entry in volume 8, number 4, on page 17 of St. Clair's *Bedford-The History and Genealogy of Bedford County, Pa.*, which is a pamphlet found in the Pioneer Library at Bedford, states that Nathan Hurley appeared on the 1850 tax duplicate, Harrison Township, Bedford County, with $523 valuation; $2.09 county tax; and $1.60 state tax. Nathan was the father of twelve children, three of whom were girls who died prior to 1850; with nine surviving, listed following:

1. Rebecca Hurley, born c.1822. Married Abraham Griffith and emigrated to Australia in 1855, of whom more.
2. William Hurley, born June 15, 1830, probably in Bedford County, Pennsylvania, died March 31, 1911; married to

Josephine Henderson. He is shown at the age of 20 in the household of his father in the 1850 census of Harrison township, Bedford County, where he was probably married. According to the *History of Bedford, Somerset and Fulton Counties, Pa.*, 1884, William enlisted September 20, 1862 in Company E, 84th Regiment, Pennsylvania Infantry, USA, for service in the War of the Rebellion. There is another entry in *History of Huntington and Blair Counties, Pennsylvania*, 1883, which states that William Hurley was mustered in April 5, 1864 and transferred to Company I, 57th Regiment, Pennsylvania Volunteers. Yet another report found in the Archives at Washington, D. C., states that he enlisted on September 20, 1862 (as above reported), but as 8th corporal in Captain Hay's Company, 154th Regiment, Pennsylvania Drafted Militia. He served in Hancock's Corps, was wounded, and discharged June 15, 1865. In *Farquhar's Directory of Bedford County*, 1886, William Hurley is listed as being the proprietor of Hurley House, a hotel in New Enterprise. He is listed in yet another book dealing with the Civil War, titled *The Soldiers of Blair County*, as having died in 1911, and buried at Greenlawn cemetery at Roaring Spring, in Blair County, Pennsylvania. His children included:

a. Arabella Hurley, born c.1853
b. Similia Hurley, born c.1855
c. Adela Hurley, born c.1857
d. Melicina Hurley, born c.1859
e. Arthamecy Hurley, born c.1861; married Parker
f. William E. Hurley, born July 26, 1864 at Broad Top, Huntington County, Pennsylvania, and died November 2, 1941 at Bellefonte. At one time, he owned a livery stable with his brother George in Phillipsburg, until he was elected sheriff of Centre County, Pa in 1910. He married Emma Replogle, who was born

January 18, 1866 and died November 18, 1947. She was a daughter of John Long Replogle (known as "Jockey John"), and Elizabeth Dull Replogle. Three daughters, and apparently an infant death son, unnamed:

(1) Helen Hurley, married Frederick F. Hallowell of Bellefonte

(2) Della Hurley, married Frederick Cory and, at the time of her mother's death, lived in Hendersonville, N. C.

(3) Hazel Hurley, who also lived at Hendersonville

(4) Son Hurley, stillbirth March 1, 1888. Buried at Maria cemetery, Bedford County, Pa

g. George Hurley, born c.1869

h. Effie Luthicia Hurley. Information found in clippings of older obituaries in Pioneer Library at Bedford, Pa. Born at Saxton January 4, 1861 and resided at Morrison's Cove. Died at St. Petersburg, Florida. The obituary names her parents and brother George, and sister Arthamecy (there called Artha), thus fixing the identify of this individual. Married to Howard Fleck, and had at least one son:

(1) Hurley Fleck, a detective in Blair County, who was married and had at least two daughters:

(a) Dorothy Fleck

(b) Elizabeth Fleck

3. Emily Hurley, born c.1832, probably in Pennsylvania. In her father's household in the 1850 census of Harrison township, Bedford County, Pa. Married to Neff and lived in Clearfield County, Pa. Reportedly appeared with her husband and family in the 1860 census of Cambria County, Pa.

4. Melcinia Hurley, born c.1834, probably in Pennsylvania. Also in the 1850 census as above, and also married to a

man named Neff, perhaps a brother of her sister Emily's husband. They also reportedly appeared in the 1860 census of Cambria County, and lived in Clearfield

5. George Hurley, born October 22, 1836, of whom more
6. Arnold Hurley, born 1839 in Pennsylvania and died 1920, according to his tombstone found at St. Johns cemetery in Albany, Oregon, by Thelma Horner Hurley, and reported to me. The stone carries his name, with dates of birth and death, and that of his wife Amanda J., who was born in 1847 and died in 1937. Arnold went west about 1861, crossing the plains by ox team and wagon, to Lassen County, California. It was there he married Amanda Jane Garrett in 1863. They appear to have had their first child, Daniel (1867) in California, and then returned for a time to Bedford County, Pa. They are found in the 1870 census of Bedford near his brother, William Hurley (1830). Their children were:
   a. Daniel Hurley, born c.1867 in California
   b. Margaret Hurley, born c.1869 in Bedford County
   c. Annie Hurley, born c.1875
   d. Blanche Hurley, born c.1878
   e. Ida Hurley, born c.1885
7. John Hurley, born c.1843. Mustered into service in Union forces on October 28, 1861. Reportedly served as private, Company F, 76th Pennsylvania Infantry, USA. Died at Fortress Monroe in Virginia, November 30, 1861. Appears to be buried at Hampton Cemetery, Va.
8. Melcissan (or Melcissary) Hurley, born c.1845, perhaps in Harrison township, Bedford County, Pa
9. Daniel Webster Hurley, born c.1846 probably in Harrison township. He enlisted on August 30, 1864 at Harrisburg, Pennsylvania as a private in Company G, 200th Regiment, Pennsylvania Infantry. The Declaration of Recruit, which he signed, indicates that he was then 18 years of age, born in Bedford County, Pa., and that he was then a

laborer. He was described as having a dark complexion, brown eyes, dark hair; he was five feet, six inches tall. His certificate of death states that he died January 30, 1865 of typho-malarial fever, contracted while in service. The certificate states that he was of Captain George Huber's Company G, 200th Regiment, Penn-sylvania Volunteers, 1st Brigade, 3rd Division, 9th Army Corps. He was said to be due five months pay at the rate of sixteen dollars per month, plus the sum of one hundred dollars retained U. S. Bounty. Other papers indicate that he died in hospital near Meade Station, in Virginia.

George Hurley
1836-1924

This son of Nathan Hurley (1798), was born October 22, 1836 at Hagerstown, Washington County, Maryland. According to his obituary, he died May 31, 1924 at the home of his daughter Mrs. Albert Kinsey, at Prairie Depot, in Wood County, Ohio, after a brief illness, and he is buried at Buffalo Mills, in Bedford County, Pennsylvania. It is also reported there that he came to Bedford County from Clearfield County, Pa. "over 56 years ago" or about c.1868. Will records of Bedford County indicate a file number of 1924-0085, which contains papers relative to his estate, including a will, which has not been researched. He was married to Mary Ann VanAllman, who was born August 12, 1837 in Blair County, Pa. and died March 5, 1916; daughter of Peter Phenalman and Nancy Myers Phenalman. (Note she apparently changed the spelling of her name in marriage records). According to *History of Bedford, Somerset and Fulton Counties, Pa.*, 1884, George moved from Clearfield County, Pa. to Harrison township and, in 1870, he located on a farm in the Buffalo Creek valley, which he had purchased from Jacob Biechner. He was listed in Farquhar's *Directory of Bedford County*, edition of 1878 and 1879, as a farmer at Buffalo Mills. He was the father of ten children:

1. Alvin Blair Hurley, born April 23, 1858 or 1859, at Buffalo Mills in Bedford County, Pa. and died March 26, 1940 of a heart attack at his home in Manns Choice, Bedford County, which occurred while he was seated in a chair in his kitchen. His obituary lists his name as Blair A. Hurley, perhaps reversing the names, although we are not positive which is correct. Wills and estate index of Bedford County lists Blair Hurley under file 1940-0159, which contains various papers relative to his estate, but no will is indicated. Married October 22, 1895 to Emma Eugenia Carpenter. She was born November 11, 1864 and died August 8, 1937, daughter of Samuel B. and Ida May Carpenter. He is listed in Farquhar's *Directory of Bedford County*, as a farmer living at Buffalo Mills. There were four children, all born in Bedford County:
    a. John Alden Hurley, born August 25, 1896 and died August 6, 1921; married to Belva Wertz. Will records of Bedford County contain papers relative to his estate filed as 1921-0132, with no will being indicated. He apparently had two children:
        (1) Harry B. Hurley, born April 9, 1918; lived just six months
        (2) Evaline Hurley, born September 5, 1919
    b. Mary Ida Hurley, born March 15, 1898 and died December 18, 1990 at Memorial Hospital in Bedford County. Buried at Milligan's Cove Christian church cemetery. Married on October 12, 1920 to Harvey A. Bohn who died June 23, 1980. They had at least four sons, one of whom predeceased his mother; ten grandchildren and ten great grandchildren. The four known sons were:
        (1) Lloyd C. Bohn, who died November 6, 1983
        (2) Harold A. Bohn

(3) Walter L. Bohn
(4) Chester R. Bohn

c. Ada Belle Hurley, born May 6, 1900 and married July 26, 1922 to Roy A. Plessinger. Lived at Amaranth c.1924
d. Laura May Hurley, born March 26, 1902 and married to Ralph Wolford. Lived in Salem, Ohio c.1924

2. Clayton B. Hurley, born 1860 in Clearfield County, Pa. Married in 1883 to Missouri Miller, who died before her husband. His obituary indicates that he died at his home in Johnstown, Pa. at the age of 75, placing his death c.1935. He had a son:
   a. George Scott Hurley, born November 23, 1883 at Connellsville and died February 5, 1967 at Hyndman, Pa. Married on September 13, 1911 to Marian W. Brown, who was born 1883 and died 1972
3. Josephine Hurley, born 1862 in Clearfield County, Pa. Married on November 22, 1882 to William H. Carpenter, who was born September 27, 1860. They lived at Buffalo Mills, and had at least three children:
   a. Blaine H. Carpenter.
   b. Fannie M. Carpenter.
   c. Ida M. Carpenter.
4. Emma Jane Hurley, born November 17, 1867 in Clearfield County, Pa. Married October 3, 1888 to George Rock, and lived at Johnstown, Pa. at the time of her father's death. In 1940, they lived at Detroit, Michigan; at least four children:
   a. Effie Rock
   b. Ralph Rock
   c. Mae Kathryn Rock, born March 27, 1900 and died September 16, 1987 at Riverside, California.
   d. Bertha Rock

5. Laura Hurley, born August 11, 1872 in Bedford County, Pa. and married May 16, 1899 to Dr. Calvin C. Dibert. The children included: Mae; Herbert; and Enfield
6. Ida Bell Hurley, born April, 1870 at Buffalo Mills, Bedford County. Married May 16, 1899 to Albert Kinsey, living at Buffalo Mills and later (c.1940) in Wayne, Ohio. Children included:
   a. Edison Kinsey, born 1900.
   b. Ruth Kinsey.
   c. Edna Kinsey.
7. Effie B. Hurley, born November 13, 1874 at Buffalo Mills. Married to Frank G. May and lived at Altoona, Pa. Their children were:
   a. Lillian May.
   b. Arthur May.
   c. Franklin May.
8. George Melvin Hurley, born c.1878 at Buffalo Mills, Pa.; died 1942 and buried at Lyberger Lutheran church cemetery, Bedford County, Pa. Married first in 1908 to Sada Viola Waugerman, who was born 1878 and died 1937; buried with her husband. He was married secondly to Myrtle Schlinger, and lived at Johnstown, Pa. Children not known.
9. William Lincoln Hurley, born August 10, 1865 in Clearfield County, Pa. and died December 3, 1939 at Covina, California. Married July 22, 1891 at Bedford to Mary Elizabeth Wilhelm. She was born March 11, 1870 in Pennsylvania and died December 30, 1947 at Hemet, California. Buried at Oakdale Memorial Park in Glendora, California with her husband. They had eight children:
   a. Albert Lincoln Hurley, born on September 1, 1892 at Manns Choice in Bedford County, Pa. Married March 26, 1915 to Louise Ruth Danker, and married second to Louise Didier. At least two daughters:

(1) May Hurley, married Clifford Atkinson
(2) Daisy Hurley, married first Wilson and second Ivan Pagh

b. Ross Byron Hurley, born February, 1894 at Manns Choice and died March 19, 1985. Married Dot Doyle and had three children:
   (1) Ross Byron Hurley, Jr.; married Pauline Hegwood. A son:
      (a) Ross Byron Hurley, III
   (2) Wallace Hurley
   (3) Rosetta Hurley

c. Cora A. Hurley, born 1895 at Manns Choice and died October 11, 1906. Buried at Milligan Cove Christian church cemetery between Manns Choice and Buffalo Mills in Bedford County, Pa.

d. Della May Hurley, born 1901 at Manns Choice; married Harry Baker

e. Walter Scott Hurley, born December 22, 1905 at Manns Choice; died February 4, 1987 at Covina, California. Married to Nina Thomas on April 15, 1935 and had a daughter:
   (1) Janis Elaine Hurley, married Richard Jones and had a son:
      (a) Revere Jones

f. Robert Lee Hurley, born December 10, 1907 at Manns Choice and married to Helen Marshall. They had children:
   (1) Susy Hurley.
   (2) Robert Lee Hurley, Jr.

g. Daisy Elizabeth Hurley, born June 24, 1911 at Covina, Los Angeles County, California. Married William Totman.

h. Thomas Blair Hurley, born March 9, 1900 at Manns Choice, Pa. and died August 12, 1966 at Covina, California. Married November 11, 1922 at Pomona,

CA to Ada Luella Ayers, born April 23, 1904 and died June 19, 1933, a daughter of Elias Lincoln Ayers and Clara Heckman Ayers. Both buried at Oakdale Memorial Park cemetery. They had children:

(1) Thomas Blair Hurley, Jr., born September 2, 1923 and married October 27, 1944 to Thelma Irene Horner. She was born July 28, 1924, daughter of Harold Horner and Radene Myers. Four children, born Covina, California:
   (a) Thomas Blair Hurley, III, born December 25, 1945 and married to Sharon Elaine McLaughlin, born April 8, 1949. Two children, born at Covina, California: Russell Wayne Hurley, who was born December 16, 1973; and Ann Michelle Hurley, born September 15, 1975.
   (b) Alan Blaine Hurley, born December 12, 1949 and married July 8, 1978 to Carol Ann DeSante
   (c) Patrick Dana Hurley, born August 18, 1952
   (d) Denise Lynn Hurley, born February 27, 1955. Married Rodney Dean Womack, born March 7, 1952, a son of Donald W. and Mary Emily Hatch Womack. Two children: Austin Charles Womack, born February 10, 1978; and Layne Elizabeth Womack, born October 3, 1980.

(2) Harlow William Hurley, born June 2, 1926. Married first to Norma Lee Noble on September 10, 1948, and second to Eileen Renslow. He had four children:
   (a) Claudia Lee Hurley, born 1950
   (b) Sheryl Annette Hurley, born 1951
   (c) Lisa Ann Hurley, born 1965

(d) Kent Hurley.

(3) Joan Louise Hurley, born December 4, 1927 and married October 10, 1948 to James R. Williams. They had two children:

(a) James Richard Williams, born 1949. Married Marilyn Miranda and had a son: Trevor.

(b) Jon Harlow Williams, also married

(4) Joyce Annette Hurley, born August 25, 1930 and married November 15, 1952 to Lawrence V. Merchep. Two children:

(a) Shelly Lee Merchap.

(b) Lynette Leigh Merchap.

(5) James Ayers Hurley, born October 27, 1932. Married to Dawn Robertson and had three children:

(a) Michael Hurley.

(b) Pamela Hurley.

(c) Jaime Hurley.

10. John R. Hurley, an infant death, who died March 29, 1883 at the age of 4 months and 25 days. Buried at Hyndman cemetery near Buffalo Mills, Pennsylvania

Rebecca Hurley
1822-1898

This daughter of Nathan Hurley (1798) and his first wife, Susan Stottlemyer Hurley (1804), was born c.1822, probably in Washington County, Maryland, or perhaps in Pennsylvania. She died June 21, 1898 in Kangerong Shire, Mornington County, Dromana District, Colony of Victoria, Australia. Rebecca met Abraham Griffith, probably in St. Joseph, Missouri, while she was on a wagon train bound for Oregon, and decided to leave the train. They were married in Blair County, Pa. c.1839, when she was about 17 years old. Abraham was master of a whaling vessel out of Philadelphia, born about 1815 in Lancaster, Pa., a son of Jonah and Elizabeth Harris Griffith. It appears that two of their children; William Harris (1842) and Sylvester (1846); were deceased prior to 1855. The rest of the family sailed aboard the *Nimrod* from New York, and arrived at Port Philip, Australia, on March 7, 1855. They settled in the Kangerong, where Abraham, together with Richard Watson, built the first house by Dunn's Creek, in the area later to become the township of Dromana.

In Australia, Abraham carried out an extensive business as a builder and contractor. He farmed Griffith's Flat near Dunn's Creek, just below the Nepean Highway, where the Dromana abattoirs originally stood. He is said to have furnished many of the 12 by 12 beams used in the construction of the Dromana pier. He and the two Eaton brothers planted extensive crops of maize. He died of injuries received when he was thrown from a horse-drawn cart on the Melbourne to Pt. Nepean Road at St. Martha. He lived for several days, but died of a brain hemorrhage on March 22, 1874, and is buried in the Dromana cemetery. Rebecca is believed to have returned to America at some time for a visit with one of her sons. She died at Dromana, however, and is buried there with her husband. They had five children, all born in Pennsylvania:

1. Arthamecey Griffith, born c.1840, of whom more
2. William Harris Griffith, born c.1842; died before 1855
3. Sylvester Griffith, born c.1846; died before 1855
4. John Calvin Griffith, born October 1, 1848, of whom more
5. Jonah Griffith, born c.1850, of whom more

Arthamecey Griffith
1840-1893

This daughter of Rebecca Hurley Griffith (1822) and Abraham Griffith (1815), was born in Pennsylvania c.1840 and immigrated to Australia with her parents in 1855. She was married twice; first in 1856 to George Bidgood, a butcher in Dromana; and second in 1868 to George Elliman, a blacksmith of Dromana. He was a son of John and Maria Mirfield Elliman and died June 15, 1911. Arthamecey died in 1893. Three children were born to each marriage, in the order listed:

1. Rebecca Bidgood, born c.1857; married William Connell
2. George Bidgood, born 1861, died February 21, 1936. Indented Head Victoria; married Margaret Patterson, born c.1865 and died November 7, 1940. At least ten children:
   a. Walter Bidgood.
   b. Jack Bidgood.
   c. Ada Bidgood.
   d. Ethel Bidgood.
   e. Florence Bidgood.
   f. George Henry Bidgood, born 1883 and died 1884
   g. William James Bidgood, born August 6, 1886, died September 16, 1971. Married Christina Maude Gunn and had children:
      (1) William John Bidgood.
      (2) Margaret Ruby Bidgood.
      (3) Marjorie Joyce Bidgood.
   h. Alice Bidgood.
   i. Albert Bidgood.
   j. Ada Doris Bidgood, born January 6, 1906
3. Walter Ernest Bidgood, married Elsie Florence, who was born c.1897 and died October 20, 1980. He died October 29, 1973, the father of two children:
   a. Phyllis Irene Bidgood, born February 23, 1920
   b. An infant death Bidgood, June 1, 1929.
4. William John Elliman, born 1869 and died 1941. Married to Ellen Patterson and had seven children:
   a. William Elliman.

b. Walter Elliman.
c. Charles Elliman.
d. Violet Elliman.
e. Isabel Elliman, married Walter Curry
f. Ian Sylvester Elliman, married Amanda Florence; three children:
   (1) Eric Elliman.
   (2) Ivan Elliman, married Barbara Mills and had two children:
      (a) Robert Elliman, married Christine
      (b) Julie Elliman.
   (3) Loris Elliman.
g. George Henry Elliman, born February 18, 1890 and married Ida, born c.1896 and died May 28, 1927. Two children:
   (1) Charles Leonard Elliman., died at 2 years and 9 months
   (2) Henry Elliman.

5. Ada Maria Elliman, born 1871 and died May 15, 1952. She was six feet, two inches tall, and known as "Big Nant." Her husband's name was not reported to me, although there were at least two children:
   a. Frederick Ernest Elliman, married Ethel Dreda Hardiman and married second to Bernie Cole; two children:
      (1) Dorothea Miriam Elliman, died at six months
      (2) Gloria Patricia Elliman, married Norman Morse and had four children:
         (a) Amanda Jane Morse.
         (b) David Morse.
         (c) Andrew Morse.
         (d) Norman Morse, Jr.
   b. Ethel Arthamecey Elliman., married William Pearson and had a son:

(1) Neal Pearson, who was married and had two children:
   (a) Glen Pearson, who married Virginia and had children.
   (b) John Pearson, who also had children.

6. Isabella Elliman, born August 10, 1875. Married to Billy Thompson of Mornington and had three children:
   a. Dulcie Thompson.
   b. Meecie Thompson.
   c. Les Thompson.

John Calvin Griffith
1848-1927

This son of Rebecca Hurley Griffith (1822) and Abraham Griffith (1815), was born October, 1848 in Pennsylvania, and moved with his parents to Australia in 1855 aboard the *Nimrod* out of New York. He was a carter and woodcutter of Dromana, and died October 9, 1927. Married April 14, 1872 Mary Dowling, born May 24, 1851 and died March 8, 1940. John Calvin reportedly gave up the Quaker faith to become a Catholic but soon rejected that after an argument with the Priest, whom he is said to have threatened with a shotgun after an argument. John Calvin was father of eleven children:

1. John Calvin Griffith, Jr., born October 21, 1873 and died December 25, 1956. He was a bachelor farmer who lived with his spinster sister Jane in Dromana. He drove the Cobb and Company coach from Dromana to Hastings for fish and then to Melbourne and return with passengers.
2. Evelyn May Griffith, born March 28, 1875 and died March 23, 1959. She was an artist; married Jack Shand.
3. Florence Griffith, born January 16, 1877 and died in her 90s. She was married to Jack Heffen and had two sons.

4. Albert Griffith, born September 12, 1878 and died August 30, 1964. He was a blacksmith and married Molly McLear. They had three children:
   a. Albert Griffith, Jr., a farmer, who died c.1980. Married Winnie Woodfred and had two children:
      (1) June Griffith, married Kevin Wooley and had two children:
         (a) Diane Wooley, born 1955, married Mike Eagles and had children: Dane Eagles, born 1979; Grant Eagles, born 1983; and Rebecca Eagles, born 1986
         (b) Beverley Wolley, married Jim Barger and had five children: William Barger; Julie Barger; Mary Jane Barger; Robert Barger; and Susan Barger.
   b. Rupert George Griffith, married Thelma and had two children:
      (1) Brian Griffith, married June Wallace and had four daughters
      (2) Joyce Griffith, married Bill Blackburn; two children:
         (a) Geoff Blackburn.
         (b) Lyn Blackburn.
   c. Vera Florence Griffith, married to Peter Gleeson
5. Mary Jane Griffith, born August 27, 1881 and died October 19, 1976
6. Kate Griffith, born September 16, 1883 and died c.1978. Married to Walter Bags and had two children:
   a. Merle Bags.
   b. Lyle Bags.
7. George Harris Griffith, born July 11, 1885; married Annie, no family
8. Charles William Griffith, born August 23, 1894 and died May 17, 1964. Married an Irish girl, Minnie; no children

9. Lillian Griffith, born November 1, 1887; married George Larkins
10. Thomas Griffith, born August 21, 1880; died September 1, 1880
11. Wilfred Griffith, born December 1, 1892 and died c.1986. Married first to Gladys Scott and second to Violet Simcox. He was a breeder of pigs until 1966; a member of several clubs, such as football; and green-keeper and life member of Somerville Bowling Club. He fought in the Boer War and in World Wars I and II. He had a child from his first marriage:
    a. Frank Griffith, married Mavis and lived at Frankston

Jonah Griffith
1850-1936

This son of Rebecca Hurley Griffith (1822) and her husband Abraham Griffith (1815), was born c.1850 in Pennsylvania, and moved to Australia with his parents in 1855 aboard the *Nimrod* out of New York. He was a carpenter, boat-builder and fisherman, and died July 23, 1936. He was married March 8, 1870 to Sarah Sawyer, who died July 12, 1933 at Dromana. They had seven children:

1. Maude Alice Griffith, born 1871 and died 1956. Single and lived in McCullough Street, Dromana, in a house built by her father
2. Edith Annie Griffith, born November 15, 1872 or 1873
3. Delilah Sarah Griffith, born August 15, 1874; moved to Sydney
4. Gertrude Griffith, born August 15, 1876; also moved to Sydney
5. Frederick George Sylvester Griffith, born October 29, 1878 and died 1958. He was a fisherman and boat-builder, and had at least nine children:
    a. Sylvester Griffith.

b. Jack Griffith.
c. Fred Griffith.
d. Aggie Griffith.
e. Enid Griffith.
f. Betty Griffith.
g. May Griffith.
h. George Griffith.
i. Ronnie. Griffith.

6. Harry Lewis Theobald Griffith, born January 23, 1885 and died March 27, 1954. Married 1911 to Millie Shergold and had four children:
   a. Leonard Griffith, born August 19, 1912 and died October 27, 1962. Married, and had two sons:
      (1) Neal Griffith.
      (2) Win Griffith.
   b. Wilbur Griffith, born 1914 and died October 22, 1968. Married to Edna and had eight children:
      (1) Janice Griffith, married Fowler
      (2) Lew Griffith, married a Greek girl, Nina
      (3) Nicky Griffith, married Les; three children:
         (a) Craig
         (b) Narelle
         (c) Dwayne.
      (4) Diane Griffith
      (5) Mitzi Griffith
      (6) Gary Griffith
      (7) Paul Griffith
      (8) Leonard Griffith
   c. Sadie Millicent Griffith, born June 15, 1916 and married May 27, 1939 to Thomas George Phillips, who died August 16, 1980. They had three children:
      (1) Joy Millicent Phillips, born December 15, 1940 and married Neal Greig; two children:
         (a) Lauren Greig
         (b) Tracey Greig.

(2) Stanley Roy Phillips, born April 28, 1942 and married to Gillian Taylor; two children:
    (a) Carolyn Emma Phillips
    (b) Sara Louise Phillips.
(3) Merle Janette Phillips, born October 2, 1944 and married April 8, 1967 to Brian Gaskell. In 1989, Merle was living at 6 Eagle Court, Dingley 3172, Melbourne, Australia, and is our correspondent. They had two children:
    (a) Kelvin Brian Gaskell: July 6, 1972
    (b) Cara Leanne Gaskell: August 10, 1975

d. Stanford Griffith, born 1921 and married to Lorma; two children:
   (1) Barry Griffith, married Kathy and had a child: Sharon, born August 31, 1969.
   (2) Beverley Griffith, married John Canazarro; two children:
       (a) Angela Canazarro: September 16, 1971
       (b) John Canazarro, Jr.: November 14, 1974.

7. Grace Dora Griffith, born 1889 and died February 25, 1977. Married to Doug Cairns and had a son:
   a. Ivan Cairns, married to Roma

Several marriages were found in the Index to Marriage Licenses, 1799-1860 at the courthouse in Hagerstown, Washington County, Maryland. Males and females are reported in the same index, and are shown here. Additionally, some miscellaneous references were found in various sources, and will be included as well. All surnames in the left column are that of Stottlemyer, or a variant spelling of the name.

Given Name	Information
A. J.	Born c.1834, died 02/16/1881, buried in the IOOF cemetery in Garrett County.

David	Md 02/17/1825 Isabella Hays
Elias	Md c.1874 to Annie Lantz Lawrence, widow of William Lawrence (1841). Elias had two children: Dessie, md Edward Harp of Cavetown; and George, married and lived in Baltimore.
Elizabeth	Md 09/02/1819 Owen Forrest
George	Md 02/08/1814 Susannah Pry
Isaiah	Md 12/30/1856 Mary Gilday
J. Newton	Md Minnie C. V. Summers, d/o David W. Summers (1840) and Annie M. Roltenheffer.
John	Md 11/19/1819 Susanna Wolf
John M.	Md 10/10/1832 Henrietta Hays
Joseph	Md 01/16/1835 Sophia Hays
Kezia	Md 10/16/1860 Jacob Harvey Ridenour, son of Jacob Ridenour and Elizabeth Flora. Parents of Nettie, who md Samuel West as his second wife; no children.
Layann	Md 09/04/1845 Jacob C. Bowers
Mahala	Md 10/23/1837 George Clevidence
Mary	Md 07/24/1822 George Lins
Sabra A.	Md 08/25/1848 Henry Farmer
Susan	Md 12/27/1858 John H. Johnson

BIBLIOGRAPHY

Adams, Katharine Beall. *Maryland Heritage-A Family History.* Hillsboro, NC Privately printed 1983

American Genealogical Research Institute. *Walker Family History,* Washington, D. C. 1972.

Andrews, Mathew Page. *Tercentary History of Maryland.* Three volumes. Chicago & Baltimore. S. J. Clarke Publishing Co. 1925.

Baltz, Shirley Vlasak. *A Chronicle of Belair.* Bowie, Md. Bowie Heritage Committee.

Barnes, Robert. *Maryland Marriages, 1634-1777*

_____. *Maryland Marriages, 1778-1800*

_____. *Marriages and Deaths From the Maryland Gazette 1727-1839.* Baltimore. Genealogical Publishing Co. 1973

_____. *Colonial Families of Anne Arundel County, Maryland.* Westminster, Maryland: Family Lines Publications, 1996.

_____. *Marriages and Deaths from Baltimore Newspapers.* Three volumes. Baltimore. Genealogical Publishing Co. 1978

Beall, Frederick Carroll. *Robert Beall, the Scotsman, Immigrant.* Privately printed booklet. 1976. Copy at Montgomery County Historical Society Library, Rockville, Md.

Bowie, Effie Gwynn. *Across The Years in Prince George's County.* Baltimore, Md. Genealogical Publishing Company. Original 1947. Reprint 1996.

Bowman, Tressie Nash. *Montgomery County Marriages, 1796-1850*

Brown, Helen W. *Index of Marriage Licenses, Prince George's County, Maryland 1777-1886.* Baltimore, Md. Genealogical Publishing Co. Reprint. 1995

_______________. *Prince George's County Maryland Indexes of Church Registers 1686-1885, Volume 2.* Westminster, Md. Family Line Publications. 1994

Brown, Ann Paxton. Personal collection of genealogical notes and abstracts; major families of Montgomery County, Maryland.

Brumbaugh. *Maryland Records.* 1915 and 1928 issues; Washington County Marriages.

________. *Maryland Records, Colonial, Revolutionary, County and Church.*
________. *Census of Maryland, 1776*
Burgert, Annette Kunselman. *Eighteenth Century Emigrants from German-Speaking Lands to North America.* Volume 1, The Northern Kraichgau. The Pennsylvania German Society. 1983
Burke, Sir Bernard, Ulster King of Arms. *The General Armory of England, Scotland, Ireland and Wales, Volume 1.* Bowie, Md. Heritage Books, Inc. 1878, Reprint 1996
______________. *The General Armory of England, Scotland, Ireland and Wales, Volume 2.* Bowie, Md. Heritage Books, Inc. 1878, Reprint 1996
______________. *The General Armory of England, Scotland, Ireland and Wales, Volume 3.* Bowie, Md. Heritage Books, Inc. 1878, Reprint 1996
Bussard, Ruthella. *The Genealogy of Peter Bossert-Bussard, 1761-1802.* Frederick, Maryland. Jeanne Bussard Workshop. 1970-1974.
Carothers, Bettie Sterling. *1776 Census of Maryland.* Westminster, Md. Family Line Publications. 1992
Carr, Lois Green; Menard, Russell R.; Peddicord, Louis. *Maryland at the Beginning.*
Cavey, Kathleen Tull-Burton. *Tombstones and Beyond, Prospect U. M. Church Cemetery and Marvin Chapel Church Cemetery.* Westminster, Maryland: Family Lines Publications, 1995
Church of Jesus Christ of Latter Day Saints. *Family group sheets, computerized ancestral files, International Genealogical Index, and other pertinent records.* Family History Center, Silver Spring, Maryland.
Clark, Edythe Maxey. *William Pumphrey of Prince George's County, Maryland, and his Descendants.* Anundsen Publishing Company. 1992.
Coldham, Peter Wilson. *The Bristol Register of Servants Sent to Foreign Plantations 1654-1686*, Genealogical Publishing Company, Baltimore. 1988
______________. *The Complete Book of Emigrants, 1607-1660,* Genealogical Publishing Co., Baltimore, 1987
Core, Earl L. *The Monongalia Story*, West Virginia: McClain

Printing Company, 1974-1984
Day, Jackson H. *The Story of the Maryland Walker Family, Including the Descendants of George Bryan Walker and Elizabeth Walker Beall.* 1957, privately printed manuscript.
Dern, John P. and Waidner, M. Marjorie. *Rauenzahner to Routson, A Family on the Move.* Picton Press, Camden, Maine. 1993
Dern, John P. and Grace L. Tracey. *Pioneers of Old Monocacy, The Early Settlement of Frederick County, Maryland 1721 to 1743.* Baltimore. Genealogical Publishing Co. 1987
Dern, John P. and Mary Fitzhugh Hitselberger. *Bridge in Time, The Complete 1850 Census of Frederick County, Maryland.* Redwood City, CA. Monocacy Book Company. 1978
Doliante, Sharon J. *Maryland and Virginia Colonials: Genealogies of Some Colonial Families.* Genealogical Publishing Co. Baltimore, Md. 1991
Drake, Paul. *Now in Our Fourth Century: Some American Families.* Bowie, Md. Heritage Books, Inc. 1994
Eader, Edith Oliver & Trudie Davis-Long. *The Jacob Engelbrecht Marriage Ledger of Frederick County, Maryland 1820-1890.* Monrovia, Md. Paw Prints, Inc. 1994.
______ ______________. *The Jacob Engelbrecht Death Ledger of Frederick County, Maryland 1820-1890.* Monrovia, Md. Paw Prints, Inc. 1995.
Ferrill, Matthew & Gilchrist, Robert. *Maryland Probate Records 1635-1777.* Volume 9.
Fleming, Bertha Ann. *The Brandenburg Family in America.* Not published; private compilation deposited with the Frederick County, Maryland, Historical Society.
Flowers, Susanne Files & Edith Olivia Eader. *The Frederick County, Maryland Will Index 1744-1946.* Monrovia, Md. Paw Prints, Inc. 1997
Fry, Joshua & Jefferson, Peter. *Map of Virginia, North Carolina, Pennsylvania, Maryland, New Jersey 1751.* Montgomery County, Md Library, Atlas Archives.
Gaithersburg, Maryland, City. *Gaithersburg, The Heart of Montgomery County.* Privately printed. 1978
Gilland, Steve. *Frederick County Backgrounds.* Westminster, Maryland: Family Lines Publications, 1995.

____________. *Early Families of Frederick County, Maryland and Adams County, Pennsylvania.* Westminster, Maryland: Family Lines Publications, 1997.

Gurney, John Thomas, III. *Cemetery Inscriptions of Anne Arundel County, Maryland. Volume 1* . Pasadena, Md. Anne Arundel Genealogical Society. 1982, 1994.

____________________. *Cemetery Inscriptions of Anne Arundel County, Maryland. Volume 2.* Chelsea, MI. BookCrafters. 1987

Haney, Ritchie Lee. *1920 Census for Damascus, Montgomery County, Maryland.* From personal notes of his father, Ritchie E. Haney, census-taker. Damascus, Md. Private. 1997

Hinke and Reinecke. *Evangelical Reformed Church, Frederick, Maryland*

Hinman-Sotcher. *Genealogies of Pennsylvania Families.* Pennsylvania Genealogical Magazine, Volume II

Holdcraft, Jacob Mehrling. *Names in Stone; 75,000 Cemetery Inscriptions From Frederick County, Maryland.* Ann Arbor, Michigan. 1966. Reprinted with "More Names in Stone" in two volumes, Genealogical Publishing Co., Baltimore, 1985

Hopkins, G. M. *Atlas of Montgomery County, Maryland.* Baltimore, Md. Garamond/Pridemark Press, Inc.

Hurley, William N., Jr. *Neikirk, Newkirk, Nikirk and Related Families. Volume 1.* Bowie, Md. Heritage Books, Inc. 1996

___________. *Neikirk, Newkirk, Nikirk and Related Families. Volume 2.* Bowie, Md. Heritage Books, Inc. 1996

___________. *Our Maryland Heritage, Book One, The Fry Families.* Bowie, Md. Heritage Books, Inc. 1994

___________. *Our Maryland Heritage, Book Two, The Walker Families.* Bowie, Md. Heritage Books, Inc. 1997

___________. *Our Maryland Heritage, Book Three, The Fulks Families.* Bowie, Md. Heritage Books, Inc. 1997

___________. *Our Maryland Heritage, Book Four, The Watkins Families.* Bowie, Md. Heritage Books, Inc. 1997

___________. *Our Maryland Heritage, Book Five, The King Families.* Bowie, Md. Heritage Books, Inc. 1997

___________. *Our Maryland Heritage, Book Book Six, The Burdette Families.* Bowie, Md. Heritage Books, Inc. 1997

__________. *Our Maryland Heritage, Book Seven, The Soper Families.* Bowie, Md. Heritage Books, Inc. 1997

__________. *Our Maryland Heritage, Book Eight, The Brandenburg Families.* Bowie, Md. Heritage Books, Inc. 1997

__________. *Our Maryland Heritage, Book Nine, The Purdum Families.* Bowie, Md. Heritage Books, Inc. 1997

__________. *Our Maryland Heritage, Book Ten, The Perry Families.* Bowie, Md. Heritage Books, Inc. 1997

Jones, Henry Z., Jr. *More Palatine Families, Some Immigrants to the Middle Colonies 1717-1776 and their European Origins.* Universal City, California. 1991

Jourdan, Elise Greenup. *The Lane Records of Prince George's County, Maryland, 1710-1717*

Lebherz, Margaret Biser Green. *Biser Family Journals, Volumes 1, 2 and 3.* Privately printed. 1991. Frederick County Library Collection.

______________. *Jacob Beyser and Family 1746-1986.* Private printing. Frederick County Historical Society Collection.

Lloyd, Richard H. *Some Descendants of Leonard Wayman, Maryland Planter, 1670 to 1721.* Privately printed pamphlet. October, 1993. Copy at Montgomery County Historical Society Library. Rockville, Md.

Malloy, Mary Gordon; Sween, Jane C.; Manuel, Janet D. *Abstract of Wills, Montgomery County, Maryland 1776-1825*

Malloy, Mary Gordon; Jacobs, Marian W. *Genealogical Abstracts, Montgomery County Sentinel, 1855-1899.* Rockville, Md. Montgomery County Historical Society. 1986.

Manuel, Janet Thompson. *Montgomery County, Maryland Marriage Licenses, 1798-1898*

Maryland State. *Archives of Maryland*, all volumes.

Maryland Hall of Records. *Wills, estates, inventories, births, deaths, marriages, deeds and other reference works relative to counties of Maryland.*

_______________. *Maryland Calendar of Wills.* All volumes.

_______________. *Maryland Historical Society Magazine.*

_______________. *Vestry Book of St. John's Episcopal Parish Church, 1689-1810.* Original.

Meyer, Mary Keysor. *Divorces and Names Changed in Maryland By Act of the Legislature 1634-1867.* Mt. Airy, Md. Pipe Creek Publications, Inc. 1991

Meyers, Margaret E. *Marriage Licenses of Frederick County (Maryland) 1778-1810, Second Edition.* Westminster, Md. Family Line Publications. 1994

Montgomery County Court Records. *Wills, inventories of estate, deeds.* Rockville, Maryland.

Montgomery County Historical Society, Rockville, Maryland. *Folder files; census, church, correspondence, newspaper, manuscripts, library, and family records.*

______. *Queen Anne Parish Records, 1686-1777*

______. *King George Parish Records 1689 - 1801*

______. *King George Parish Records 1797-1878*

______. *St. Paul's at Baden, Parish Records*

______. *Frederick County Maryland Marriage Licenses*

______. *Montgomery County Marriages*

______. *1850 Census, Montgomery County, Maryland*

______. *1860 Census, Montgomery County, Maryland*

______. *1850 Census, Prince George's County, Maryland*

______. *1850 Census, Frederick County, Maryland*

______. *Pioneers of Old Monocacy*

______. *Mt. Olivet Cemetery, Frederick, Md.* Computer printout of burial records.

Mormon Church, Genealogical Library. Archival family group sheets and other records.

________. *International Genealogical Index.* North Carolina, Tennessee, Maryland, Pennsylvania, Ohio, Kentucky, Alabama, Virginia and other states.

Morrow and Morrow. *Marriages of Washington County, Maryland, An Index, 1799-1866.* DAR library, Washington, D. C.

Myers, Margaret Elizabeth. *Marriage Licenses of Frederick County, Maryland 1778-1810.* Westminster, Md. Family Line Publications. Second Edition, 1994

__________. *Marriage Licenses of Frederick County, Maryland 1811-1840.* Family Line Publications. 1987

__________. *Marriage Licenses of Frederick County, Maryland 1841-1865.* Family Line Publications. 1988

_________. *George Zimmerman and Descendants of Frederick County, Maryland 1714-1987.* Family Line Publications. 1987.

National Genealogical Society Quarterly. Volume 72, Number 3

Newman, Harry Wright. *Anne Arundel Gentry, A Genealogical History of Some Early Families of Anne Arundel County, Maryland. Volume One.* Annapolis, Md. Privately printed.

__________________. *Anne Arundel Gentry, A Genealogical History of Some Early Families of Anne Arundel County, Maryland. Volume Two.* Annapolis, Md. Privately printed.

__________________. *Anne Arundel Gentry, A Genealogical History of Some Early Families of Anne Arundel County, Maryland. Volume Three.* Annapolis, Md. Private printing. 1979

__________________. *Charles County Gentry.* Baltimore, Md. Genealogical Publishing Co. 1971 and 1990 reprints from 1940 original publication.

__________________. *Mareen Duvall of Middle Plantation.* Private printing 1952. Baltimore, Md. Port City Press, Inc. Reprint 1984

Omans, Donald James and Nancy West. *Montgomery County Marriages 1798-1875.* Maryland.

Peden, Henry C., Jr. *Revolutionary Patriots of Prince George's County 1775-1783.* Westminster, Md. Family Line Publications. 1997

Powell, John W. *Anne Arundel County, Maryland Marriage Records 1777-1877.* Pasadena, Md. Anne Arundel Genealogical Society. 1991

Prince George's County, Md Genealogical Society. *Index to the Probate Records of Prince George's County, Maryland, 1696-1900.* Bowie, Md. 1989.

__________. *Prince George's County Land Records, Volume A, 1696-1702.* Bowie, Maryland, 1976

__________. *1850 Census, Prince George's County, Maryland.* Bowie, Maryland, 1978

__________. *1828 Tax List Prince George's County, Maryland.* Bowie, Maryland, 1985.

Reinton, Louise Joyner. *Prince George's County, Md. Piscataway or St. John's Parish (now called King George's Parish. Index to Register, 1689-1878.*

Remsberg, Reverend W. L. *Genealogy of the Remsberg Family in America.* The Valley Register, Middletown, Md. 1912

Richardson, Hester Dorsey. *Side-lights on Maryland History, with Sketches of Early Maryland Families.* Cambridge, Md. Tidewater Publishers. 1967

Rohrbaugh, Lewis Bunker. *Rohrbach Genealogy.* Dando-Schaff Printing & Pub. Co. Philadelphia. 1970

Russell, Donna Valley. *Western Maryland Genealogy.* Volumes 1 thru 12. Catoctin Press, Middletown, Md. 1985-1996

Sargent. *Stones and Bones, Cemetery Records of Prince George's County, Maryland.*

Scharff, J. Thomas. *History of Maryland.* Three Volumes. Hatboro, Pennsylvania. Tradition Press. 1967

______________. *History of Western Maryland, Volume 1.* Baltimore, Md. Genealogical Publishing Co., Inc. 1995

______________. *History of Western Maryland, Volume II.* Baltimore, Md. Genealogical Publishing Co., Inc. 1995

______________. *History of Western Maryland, Index to Volumes I and II.* By Helen Long (which see). Baltimore, Md. Genealogical Publishing Co., Inc. 1995

Schildknecht, Calvin E. *Monocacy and Catoctin, Volumes 1 thru 111.* Gettysburg, Pa. 1994

Skinner, V. L., Jr. *Abstracts of the Prerogative Court of Maryland, 1726-1729*

Tombstone Records. *Bethesda United Methodist Church, Browningsville, Maryland. Forest Oak Cemetery, Gaithersburg, Maryland. Goshen United Methodist Church (now Goshen Mennonite Church), Laytonsville, Maryland. St. Paul's Methodist Church, Laytonsville, Maryland.*

Torrence, Clayton. *Virginia Wills and Administrations, 1632-1800.* Baltimore, Maryland: Genealogical Publishing Co., 1978

Tracey, Grace L. and Dern, John P. *Pioneers of Old Monocacy, The Early Settlement of Frederick County, Maryland 1721 to 1743.* Baltimore. Genealogical Publishing Co. 1987

Unknown Author. *Biographical Record of Washington County, Maryland.* Hagerstown public library.

VanHorn, R. Lee. *Out of the Past.*

Wampler, Roy H. *The Derr Family 1750-1986.* Gateway Press, Inc. Baltimore, Md. 1987

Warfield, J. D. *The Founders of Anne Arundel and Howard Counties, Maryland.* Baltimore. Kohn & Pollock. 1905

Washington County, Maryland. Folder files of the County Historical Society; correspondence and family records; courthouse records of wills, estates, deeds, births, deaths and marriages.

Washington County, Maryland Library. *Church Records, Zion Reformed Church at Hagerstown.*

Weiser, Frederick Sheely. *Records of Marriages and Burials in the Monocacy Church in Frederick County, Maryland, and in the Evangelical Lutheran Congregation in the City of Frederick, 1743-1811.* National Genealogical Society. 4th Printing, 1993

Welsh, Luther W., A.M., M.D. *Ancestral Colonial Families, Genealogy of TheWelsh and Hyatt Families of Maryland and Their Kin.* Lambert Moon Printing Co., Independence, Missouri. 1928.

Western Maryland Genealogy. *Frederick County (Md) Wills, Unprobated Wills, Will Book A1, 1744-1777.* Middletown, Md.

Wilcox, Shirley Langdon. *1828 Tax List Prince George's County, Maryland.* Prince George's County Genealogical Society. Special Publication No. 6. 1985

____________________. *1850 Census Prince George's County, Maryland.* Prince George's County Genealogical Society. Special Publication No. 4. 1978

____________________. *Prince George's County Land Records Volume A, 1696-1702.* . Prince George's County Genealogical Society Special Publication No. 3. 1976

____________________. *Index to the Probate Records of Prince George's County, Maryland 1696-1900.* . Prince George's County Genealogical Society. 1988

Williams, T. J. C. & Folger McKinsey. *History of Frederick County, Maryland, Volume 1.* Baltimore, Md. Genealogical Publishing Co., Inc. 1997

_______________________________. *History of Frederick County, Maryland, Volume 2.* Baltimore, Md. Genealogical Publishing Co., Inc. 1997

Williams, Thomas J. C. *History of Washington County, Maryland, Volume 1.* . Baltimore, Md. Genealogical Publishing Co., Inc. 1992

_______________. *History of Washington County, Maryland, Volume 2.* Baltimore, Md. Genealogical Publishing Co., Inc. 1992

Wright, F. Edward. *History of Washington County, Maryland, Index to Volumes 1 and 2.* Westminster, Md. Family Line Publications. 1992, 1995

____________. *Maryland Militia, War of 1812.*

____________. *Newspaper Abstracts of Frederick County, 1816 to 1819.* Westminster, Maryland: Family Lines Publications, 1993.

____________. *Marriages and Deaths in the Newspapers of Frederick and Montgomery Counties, Maryland. 1820-1830.* Westminster, Maryland: Family Lines Publications, 1992.

____________. *Anne Arundel County Church Records of the 17th and 18th Centuries.* Westminster, Md. Family Line Publications. 1989, 1994

______________. *Maryland Eastern Shore Vital Records, Book 1, 1648-1725.* Westminster, Md. Family Line Publications. 1993

______________. *Maryland Eastern Shore Vital Records, Book 2, 1726-1750.* Westminster, Md. Family Line Publications. 1993

______________. *Maryland Eastern Shore Vital Records, Book 3, 1751-1775.* Westminster, Md. Family Line Publications. 1993

______________. *Maryland Eastern Shore Vital Records, Book 4, 1776-1800.* Westminster, Md. Family Line Publications. 1994

______________. *Maryland Eastern Shore Vital Records, Book 5, 1801-1825.* Westminster, Md. Family Line Publications. 1994

INDEX

All names appearing in the text have been indexed, with reference to each page on which they appear. Most names are accompanied by a date, generally indicating date of birth, in order to differentiate between individuals having the same given name. In some cases where birth dates are not available, dates of marriage or death will appear, such as m/1825 or d/1876. In the case of common names such as John or Mary, where no date is specified, the references are without question to more than one individual. Land grant names will be listed in italics.

—C—

—D—

—H—

—I—

—J—

—K—

—N—

—O—

—P—

—Q—

—R—

—S—

—T—

—V—

—W—

CPSIA information can be obtained at www.ICGtesting.com
Printed in the USA
LVOW05s0212011214

416387LV00011B/113/P

9 780788 409233